Carla Francis is a writer whose work has been extensively featured across the UK and Australia, including on ABC and SBS radio, in the *Daily Telegraph*, *Herald Sun*, the *Courier-Mail*, *Dogs Life*, *Gold Coast Bulletin* and *CatWorld*. She has also contributed to the *Japan Times*.

THE ZEN OF CAT

An A—z of Japanese feline philosophy

CARLA FRANCIS

MACMILLAN
Pan Macmillan Australia

Pan Macmillan acknowledges the Traditional Custodians of country throughout Australia and their connections to lands, waters and communities. We pay our respect to Elders past and present and extend that respect to all Aboriginal and Torres Strait Islander peoples today. We honour more than sixty thousand years of storytelling, art and culture.

First published 2023 in Macmillan by Pan Macmillan Australia Pty Ltd
1 Market Street, Sydney, New South Wales, Australia, 2000

A catalogue record for this
book is available from the
National Library of Australia

Typeset in 12/17pt Minion Pro by Midland Typesetters, Australia

Printed by IVE
Illustrations by istockphoto

We advise that the information contained in this book does not negate personal responsibility on the part of the reader for their own health and safety. It is recommended that individually tailored advice is sought from your healthcare or medical professional. The publishers and their respective employees, agents and authors, are not liable for injuries or damage occasioned to any person as a result of reading or following the information contained in this book.

The authors and the publisher have made every effort to contact copyright holders for material used in this book. Any person or organisation that may have been overlooked should contact the publisher.

The paper in this book is FSC® certified.
FSC® promotes environmentally responsible,
socially beneficial and economically viable
management of the world's forests.

To Gershwin, a very special cat.

Contents

Introduction: Purr-logue

Domesticated cats have roamed the earth for millennia, sitting beside the ancient Pharaohs of Egypt on their golden thrones and being the pampered pets of Emperor Uda in Imperial Japan. And as times change, so too have cats – the breeds, sizes and roles that felines play in our lives.

These enigmatic creatures have a long history in the Land of the Rising Sun, dating back to the arrival of Buddhism via China in the sixth century. At that time, the main role of these *neko* (猫) was to stop pesky vermin from damaging the precious scriptures. Since then, they have truly become part of the culture. But what can we learn from these philosophical felines?

In Japanese folklore, cats are said to have special powers and are celebrated for bringing good fortune. They are so deeply embedded in the culture, several Shinto shrines and Buddhist temples are devoted to felines, such as Gōtoku-ji, located in Tokyo, said to be the birthplace of the *maneki-neko* (waving cat figurine); and Nekojinja on the small island of Tashirojima (also known as Cat Island).

Wherever you are in Japan, it won't be long before you find something fantastically feline, from fashion to folklore and everyday expressions like *nekojita* (literally 'cat's tongue', figuratively a tongue that's sensitive to heat) and *neko baba* (literally 'cat's poop', figuratively 'embezzle'). From *maneki-neko*'s beckoning paw seen in businesses across the country to the more recent Shigoto Neko, a feline mascot that warns Japanese workers about workplace safety, cats are ubiquitous in Japan.

With all that cats have seen and experienced, it's easy to imagine the knowledge these magical moggies hold; over the centuries, they have gleaned their wisdom through residing in ancient temples, and coexisting with artists, courtesans, monks and writers alike. Since cats cannot speak, during my research for this book I consulted a number of Japanese experts who share their lives with cats.

It's these mindful 'mewsings' on life that we will explore in this philosophical A–Z. Cats are great examples of how to live, as they seem free from worry and able to maintain an enviable equilibrium – rarely do we see these mystical creatures wobble. The aim of this book is to share reflective ruminations for every letter of the alphabet, beginning with *annei* (peace) and continuing all the way through to *zazen* (sitting meditation). While some words can't be directly translated into English, the Japanese language is full of subtle nuances that say much about the culture in which it originated, and holds many valuable insights.

Not only can feline sages teach us to become a little more Zen each day by showing us how to slow down, be more present and not worry too much about what others are thinking, but their love of adventure can also take us outside and allow us to reconnect with nature in a feline form of forest bathing, while their uninhibited demeanour helps us stop *cat*astrophising and encourages us to approach life with greater confidence. Just as we can train a cat, if we're truly open we can learn something from our feline companions too. After all, they've left their mark on history, playing different roles over the centuries. Perhaps Japanese cats carry the wisdom and knowledge you yearn for. As Eckhart Tolle once said, 'I have lived with several Zen masters – all of them cats.'

It's important to note that many ideas in this book, while inspired by Japan, take a Western perspective. While I have made every effort to ensure the accuracy of the content through consultation with many Japanese people during the writing process, and to show consideration for the Japanese language, culture, people and environment, at times I have given the material my own imaginative spin.

So let's journey through this A to Z of Japanese words and take inspiration from the concepts that make Japanese culture so beguiling while also gaining a fresh feline *purr*-spective on life from Japanese cats. Take me by the paw as we delve deeper into the wonderful world of Japan and see what we can learn from ancient traditions and influential animals.

I hope this book inspirates you to take your own leap of faith and become the *purr*-son you've always dreamt of being.

A

Annei 安寧
Peace and tranquillity

Have you ever wondered why the felines in Japan's cat cafes appear so purr-fectly poised and well behaved? This may be the concept the Japanese refer to as *annei* at work.

Annei has a range of meanings, most of which are commonly associated with composure, peacefulness and calm. The word relates to the attitude of the general population, who want to avoid any possible problems or conflicts and who consider someone who destabilises order a threat to society. It's one of those words, however, that many Japanese have difficulty explaining, largely due to its various implications and less common use in modern language. But *annei* is mostly assigned to situations involving public peace and conflict avoidance.

Public peace is an important aspect of Japanese culture. Whether you are at a crowded station or a roaring football match, this notion of calm is one that permeates life in Japan. Even the furry felines in Japan's bustling cat cafes embrace it.

In fact, *annei* is so deeply embedded in Japanese culture that its sentiments are woven into segments of the imperial constitution. Article 28 of the imperial constitution says: 'Japanese subjects shall, within limits not prejudicial to peace and order, and not antagonistic to their duties as subjects, enjoy freedom of religious belief'. The phrase 'and not antagonistic to their duties as subjects' intricately highlights the importance of peacekeeping among citizens, and the cultural responsibility felt by the Japanese people. And, of course, Japanese cats.

Japan's post-war constitution also prohibits the use of force and disallows Japan from maintaining any type of military. Instead, it has the Self-Defense Force (SDF), which carries out various activities including peacekeeping missions, demonstrating Japan's commitment to peace at both an individual and governmental level. This is, of course, unsurprising given Japan's non-peaceful role in World War II and the devastating consequences of the atomic bombs that ended it in 1945.

So what can we learn about peace from the Japanese and their cats? First, let's reflect on the historical concept of peace in the mountainous prefecture of Tochigi, home to the popular tourist destination Nikkō. This small city is famous for, among other things, its Tōshō-gū Shrine, and in particular the carving of the Three Wise Monkeys nestled over its door. Their playful poses adorably encapsulate the esteemed adage 'See no evil, hear no evil, speak no evil.' The shrine is also home to *Nemuri-neko*, one of Japan's most beloved national treasures – which just so happens to be feline.

Nemuri-neko: The Sleeping Cat

Have you ever longed to be as peaceful as a sleeping cat? Only about 20 centimetres long, *Nemuri-neko* is a wooden carving depicting a conked-out kitty, and is a national treasure in Japan. *Nemuri* translates to 'sleeping' but also 'peaceful', and *neko* of course means 'cat'.

Perhaps legendary Japanese sculptor Jingorō Hidari yearned for the peace of a sleeping cat when designing *Nemuri-neko*. It's said that he was so fascinated with felines that he spent many months studying them as a way to capture their movements and personalities.

Interestingly, on the other side of the Tōshō-gū gate from *Nemuri-neko* is a carved sparrow. Ordinarily these birds would be prey to a cat, but their side-by-side portrayal within the shrine is yet another symbol of peace. Since the cat is sleeping, the sparrows are safe from harm, promoting again the ideology of living harmoniously and without conflict.

Peace Poles

Given there are more than 200,000 Peace Poles in many countries all over the world, you may have come across one of these monuments on your travels. Each pole bears the words 'May Peace Prevail on Earth', inscribed in different languages on each of its four or six sides.

The idea of Peace Poles originated with Japanese philosopher and peace activist Masahisa Goi in 1955. After the traumatic events of World War II, Goi longed for global peace, so he established Byakkō Shinkō Kai, an organisation to promote spirituality and spiritual practices dedicated to world peace. He studied the teachings of various religions, including the words of Chinese founder of philosophical Taoism Lao-Tzu, and the Bible. Goi urged people to seek inner peace as well as world peace and once said: 'In order for each of us to be truly happy, the world must be at peace. Individual happiness and world peace are one and the same.'

Interestingly, the Japanese word *heiwa* is written on the side of the Peace Poles rather than *annei*. Although the two words have very similar meanings, *heiwa* is more commonly used than *annei* these days. In fact, *annei* can sound rather old-fashioned – more likely found in the classic books of Sōseki Natsume, famed novelist of the Meiji period (1868–1912) whose works include *I Am a Cat* and *Tower of London*, than in the contemporary magic realism of a Haruki Murakami novel.

Heiwa has become more commonly used since the Meiji period, when the country became embroiled in international geopolitical power relations. It corresponds with the word 'peace' in European languages.

Paper cranes

Another instantly recognisable symbol of peace in Japan is the paper crane, or *orizuru*. Cranes have long appeared in Japanese art, but they are most widely associated with the devastating aftermath of the atomic bombs dropped on Hiroshima and Nagasaki.

Yuka Nakamura, an origami teacher originally from Tokyo but now living in Queensland, Australia, teaches schoolchildren the art of paper folding. She says that 'according to the Japanese legend *Senbazuru*, anyone with the persistence to fold 1000 paper cranes will be granted their wish.' Yuka adds that 'the origin of cranes being a symbol of longevity most likely comes from the Japanese saying "Cranes live for 1000 years and turtles 10,000 years".' Although origami is no longer widely taught in schools in Japan, it is still commonly practised by school-aged kids. It is thought to reduce stress by allowing the creator to become more mindful of what is happening in the moment.

The day the atomic bomb was dropped on Hiroshima in 1945, two-year-old Sadako Sasaki was exposed to radiation and developed leukaemia as a result. Inspired by the story of *Senbazuru*, Sadako folded paper cranes as a form of therapy.

Today, a statue stands tall in Hiroshima memorialising the child victims of the bomb. Known as the Children's Peace Monument, it depicts Sadako Sasaki at the very top of the bronze statue holding a paper crane above her head. Underneath the structure, suspended from a traditional peace bell, is another bronze crane that acts as a tranquil wind chime.

This popular tourist destination is an important reminder for people to continue their endeavours to preserve peace between nations. In recent years, a steel origami crane has been erected in Kaiseizan Park, Kōriyama, Fukushima. It represents a powerful message of peace in the face of disaster. No one will ever forget the tragic scenes of the 2011 Tōhoku earthquake and tsunami, which triggered the meltdown at the Fukushima Daiichi Nuclear Power Plant and caused approximately 20,000 human deaths. The steel crane, welded from World Trade Center debris, was donated to Japan in 2012 by the September 11th Families' Association, and acts as a strong reminder of hope.

While the fortunate among us live in peaceful

countries without war or conflict, that does not necessarily mean we have inner peace. Our minds can be so busy with to-do lists, personal conflicts at work or at home, and constant worry about the increasing cost of living that we could be forgiven for not finding peace within ourselves.

The cat monks of Kyoto

Not everyone gets to wear a *rakusu*, a traditional Japanese garment worn around the neck of Zen Buddhists and usually reserved for those who have taken the precepts, but the head cat monk at Nyan Nyan Ji Temple takes the role seriously.

Nestled in the outskirts of northern Kyoto is Nyan Nyan Ji Temple, also known as Meow Meow Shrine. It is the purr-fect place to learn about peace and spirituality from a feline perspective, surrounded by the art, statues and symbols of a cat version of the bodhisattva created by founder and temple painter Tōru Kaya in 2016. One of my favourite images featured at the temple is of Kannon, the Goddess of Mercy and Compassion, also known as Avalokiteshvara in India, or Guan Yin in China, depicted in feline form with multiple arms. Kannon is well known throughout Japan as the keeper of peace and reliever of troubles. This kitty bodhisattva may indicate that cats also have the potential for enlightenment (whatever a cat's enlightenment might look like).

Speaking of what cats can teach us about peace and living harmoniously together, the owner of the cat monk, Tōru Hashimoto, told me, 'Since a cat's lifespan is much shorter than our own, stray cats, who have even shorter lifespans due to their harsh lifestyles, when we humans welcome them into our family and watch their life seriously, can teach us a lot of important things that are applicable to the life of a human being. We can learn all about love, joy, comfort and sorrow. But, strangely enough, our anger becomes much less frequent. If many people can learn these things, their hearts will overflow with kindness, and there will be less strife and hatred in the world.'

Cats are known for their ability to heal; their purrs are thought to lower stress levels, among various other therapeutic benefits. Tōru-san (the *san* is added to Japanese names to indicate respect) explains the benefits our kitty companions give us. 'I think cats who live with people are very self-assertive,' he said. 'Their casual gestures and subtle sense of distance are very attractive and healing for us. It's like the relationship between two lovers.'

The former Head Cat Priest at Nyan Nyan Ji was the green-eyed Koyuki, a wise white stray cat that was not afraid of changes in her living environment, loud noises, typhoons and earthquakes – or proudly wearing prayer beads and customised robes. Tōru-san added, 'She was very friendly to humans and treated everyone kindly, never scratching anyone in anger. Since she was such a peaceful feline, Koyuki was chosen as the first cat priest of

Nyan Nyan Ji Temple, and many people from all over the world came to see her. She was very much loved by many people.' Tōru-san continued, 'It is said that when someone with a sixth sense comes into contact with Koyuki, she will convey the power that makes people happy.'

Yukimi, like Koyuki, is a former stray cat, and is the new moggie monk in waiting. At only about four months old, Yukimi doesn't yet have any special training as an apprentice cat priest, but she's learning the ropes quickly, and always accompanies Tōru on his visits to shrines and temples. Tōru-san explained why cats make good monks: 'Unlike other animals, many people find cats to be very mysterious in their eyes and gestures. In ancient Egypt, a cat goddess named Bastet was worshipped. So it may be a very natural flow that cats who are close to God are chosen as priests.'

Finally, I asked Tōru-san about the significance of the Cat Kannon statue. He said, 'Cat Senju-kannon [Cat Thousand-armed Avalokiteshvara] is a Buddha who uses its many limbs to save many people and cats suffering in this world. I am learning the happiness of living through them.'

Finding inner peace and avoiding the cat-cophony

Who wouldn't want to be as blissed out as one of those world-famous red-faced macaques at Jigokudani Monkey

Park, as they soak themselves gleefully in the hot springs of Nagano? But how do we learn about inner peace in a world with so much commotion, in the same way Tōru learns about happiness through his cat monks?

Our minds are often perpetually rooted in the events of the past or looking wistfully towards the future rather than enjoying the here and now. And more often than not it appears that many of us have the tendency to react negatively to small snags in our day. Whether we missed the bus, received some criticism at work or were granted a rather contemptuous unsolicited comment, our reactions are often antagonistic. How does a cat react when times get tough? The kitty doesn't get angry or take things personally; it just moves out of the way and continues on. If we simply stop overthinking and gracefully allow minor bugbears to pass us by, we can achieve more peace and calm in our lives. Just as a dog tenaciously locks onto a meaty bone, humans latch onto their own thoughts. But failing to see beyond a triggered mind can be a cause for unhappiness. The trick is to catch yourself when you're doing it. As the Zen proverb goes, 'Be master of mind rather than mastered by mind.'

*

A purring kitty seems content with most things, only in a rush should they see a bird or a mouse but otherwise spending the majority of their time relishing in the most wonderfully restful snoozes. What can we learn from these seemingly untroubled creatures so that we can become more peaceful ourselves? How can we emulate their tranquil traits? One change we could make is mindfulness. Even as we approach our daily tasks – whether that's cleaning out the kitty litter or grooming our best friend – actively trying to bring our mind back to the task at hand can be hugely beneficial. Often, as we embark on our daily trials, we get in the habit of thinking we can relax only when all the chores are done, and we switch our minds over to our perceived future as we aimlessly undertake our responsibilities. But given that additional tasks are likely to emerge as our day progresses, it's in our best interests to enjoy each moment as it comes and keep our mind in the present. Cats are a constant reminder to live more in the moment and be more peaceful.

B

Bimbōshō 貧乏性
Poor man's mind

Are you the cat that gets the cream? Or is your dish always half empty? If it's the latter, you could have what the Japanese refer to as *bimbōshō*. The direct English translation of this word is 'miserly nature', but generally, *bimbōshō* is a term for what the Japanese refer to as 'poor man's mind'. It's not a word for a selfish individual or someone unwilling to part with money; rather, *bimbōshō* is more accurately assigned to those with a pessimistic outlook. No matter how much you have or what you achieve, if you have a poor man's mind you'll be constantly worried about small things and you'll struggle to feel the joy of your successes. Your accomplishments might feel empty or inconsequential, your possessions may never be enough, and ultimately you may be left feeling perpetually incomplete, no matter what opportunities come your way.

Like us, cats can demonstrate optimistic or pessimistic attitudes, depending on their nature. The more exuberant kitty is fuelled by their optimism, leaping out of their basket each morning with their ears pricked as they race down the corridor of life, full of inquisitive anticipation for each new day. These carefree cats might get caught performing perilous trapeze acts on the neighbour's fence or lunging after lizards on busy streets, taking life by the whiskers and developing their skills. In contrast, the more pessimistic puss may be less adventurous, constrained by their need to feel safe and avoid dangerous situations. This is the type of cat that misses every family holiday because the car conjures up too many traumatic flashbacks to previous vet visits. Sure, these risk-averse kitties are probably less prone to catfights, and most of us are well versed in the saying 'Curiosity killed the cat', but the Japanese also have a saying: 'A cat that's always mewing doesn't catch mice.' If we find fault with everything that comes across our path, how will we ever be able to enjoy what life has to offer us? The original meaning of this saying is: people who talk a lot don't do much. So it's better to stop the negative chitchat and get on with things, avoid those people who bring us down, and move forward.

Concerning ourselves with too many trivialities is not good for us and will hamper our progress.

It's true that no matter where we go dark clouds can follow us, and even the best of us can miss those silver linings. Imagine you're on a dream holiday in a tropical resort. Now picture that guest, you know the one, with the list of complaints that stretches longer than the plane ride there. The towels aren't soft enough, the lift near the room is too noisy, the toast at the breakfast buffet wasn't warm enough. Is that guest usually you? Or are you complaining about the difficult guest who never seems to be satisfied? Either way, both parties aren't truly experiencing their holiday. Instead, the focus is on what's lacking, rather than what's there. When things don't meet our expectations, it's easy to feel disheartened and compelled to instil change.

We'll touch more on expectations later in Chapter O: *Oubaitōri*, but for now, let's look at perspective. Perception is reality, and if we're constantly scanning for inconveniences and disruptions, we'll keep finding them and our reality might start looking inconsolably bleak. But what if instead of focusing on what isn't right, we could shift our point of view and do what we can to count the wins?

Studies show that people who think more positively could enjoy myriad health benefits, including fewer strokes and longer life expectancy. So it goes without saying that improving our way of seeing the world is something we should all work towards.

It's all about purr-spective

Although cats and humans can both be optimistic and pessimistic, it's a very human trait to overcomplicate things and make more of them than necessary. We're desperate to improve, always wanting things to be optimal, but life is complicated, and we can't change everything all at once. Like a skittish kitty bouncing around on its leash, it's easy for us to get tangled in knots as we try to navigate our problems. But perhaps if we were to simplify our lives as cats so elegantly do, we might find that things aren't so bad after all. Famed Japanese novelist Sōseki Natsume wrote in the early 1900s about the complexities of people compared with cats in his novel *I Am A Cat*.

> Cats are truly simple. If we want to eat, we eat; if we want to sleep, we sleep; when we are angry, we are angry utterly; when we cry, we cry with all the desperation of extreme commitment to our grief.

If we have the habit of assuming the worst in the interest of self-preservation, we may prepare ourselves for failure and disappointment, convincing ourselves that we're not pessimists, simply realists. But when we can't allow ourselves to enjoy the things we've achieved or savour the good times because we're always worrying about finances, or complaining about work or other family members, we might feel like there's a constant barrage of negativity in our house. In fact, what we might even be doing is living like we're poor even though we're not – 'like *bimbōshō*', as the Japanese say – and viewing the world with a poor man's mind.

In the end, it's a choice to accept that sometimes things in life may not always go our way while being safe in the knowledge that these negative moments pass just the same way as the good moments in life. The real question is do we want to stay the injured stray, bottle-fed and broken, constantly worried, unable to venture far, or do we want to heal ourselves and become the pedigree show cat that wears their life's achievements with pride?

How to be less *bimbōshō*

Aimi Kojima, a fellow feline fanatic and a leader of several self-care and healing groups in Japan, suggests the following for finding more acceptance in your life: 'Embracing the gift of winter is the only way we can invite spring to flourish. A short yet passionate summer and a longer harvest in autumn means you cannot enjoy each season without the other repeatedly, as it is not the universal law in nature. If you do, you will be out of harmony and have to pay in the long term. We need to accept all seasons in our life, in ourselves, as each one of the seasons has important roles. Follow all the seasons as they are, don't push them away or try to make them stay longer. Accept it as it is. Embrace what it gives you, humbly. This is the only way we can live sustainably and keep our authenticity.'

The next chapter is where we'll really dive into harmony and balance, but it's important to recognise that sometimes even the most frustrating times in our lives can be of benefit to us and even open the door to something special. By accepting these difficult times and maintaining the knowledge that they serve as the perfect backdrop for highlighting the good times, we can alter our perspective and begin to push away that pesky poor man's mind.

Attracting abundance

Much has been written in recent years on the art of attracting abundance. There's even a bounty of life coaches who specialise in it, charging an enviable hourly fee to assist you in reaching your full potential and manifesting the life you deserve. But can we really create the opportunities we want if we never feel worthy of them?

If you've ever visited or seen photos of Japan, you're likely to have seen *ema* hanging up at shrines and in some temples. These small wooden plaques often portray images or symbols from the Zodiac calendar, and on the reverse side a message to a higher power. Traditionally, Shinto and Buddhist worshippers would use *ema* to write prayers or personal wishes on, hanging them at the shrine in the hope that the deities would grant their wish.

Nowadays, visitors to Japan can do the same, declaring their hopes and dreams on the back of the *ema*, a bit like a vision board but with words. During special events, these plaques are ritually burned, symbolising the deliverance of the writer's message.

For cat lovers, a visit to Gōtoku-ji Temple (also known as Cat Temple) in Tokyo is a must because you can not only learn about the history of the *maneki-neko* (the familiar beckoning cat figurine) but also get to write your wish on a cat-themed *ema* and hang it at the shrine. Dating back to the seventeenth century, the *maneki-neko* is known throughout Japan for bringing good luck, prosperity and wealth to the owner, and can also be found outside businesses or homes to welcome good luck inside. The story goes that a penniless monk once lived on the site of the temple with his pet cat. When a travelling feudal lord was passing through the area during a severe storm, he stopped to take shelter after he spotted a cat waving its paw and beckoning him inside the temple. As this happened, lightning struck where he'd been standing, and so the kitty had saved the lord's life. In gratitude, the lord became a patron of the temple, and in doing so brought the once struggling temple prosperity. Today, people visiting the temple make offerings because it's thought that if you leave a *maneki-neko* behind your wishes come true.

Another Japanese custom for encouraging dream manifestation includes Tanabata, a celebration on the seventh day of the seventh month. This involves people making a wish, writing it on strips of paper, and then tying that paper to a bamboo tree. The Japanese also have scores of amulets and fortune-bearing charms to aid in attracting abundance, such as the wallet charm, which is often in the form of – you guessed it – the beckoning cat.

5 tips for being less *bimbōshō*

Try to encourage more positivity and avoid the poor man's mind by incorporating the following strategies into your life:

1. **Stop catastrophising!** Don't only prepare for failure and disappointment or anticipate the worst. Good things can be just around the corner. Predicting negative events in the future is a bit like thinking you know what will happen before it occurs. If you have a cat, this might be always expecting them to wake you at 5 am, bring in a mouse or pee on your couch when the chances are they won't.

2. **Celebrate your achievements.** Make time to celebrate your successes, no matter how big or small they are. You might do this by having dinner out somewhere nice or organising a get-together with good friends.

3. **Try journalling.** Whenever something negative comes up for you, try writing down your reaction to it. Are the words you use positive or negative? Are you overly self-critical? Think about the words you use for cats. Are you softer to

felines than yourself? Most probably. Try reframing your language so it's kinder.

4. **Treat yourself.** While you mightn't live near a Japanese bath house where you can soak all your worries away, you can do small things to create happiness in your day-to-day life – like book yourself into a day spa that has a jacuzzi or steam room, buy yourself flowers, or burn some essential oils.

5. **Focus on the positive.** This might be easier said than done, but really consider whether your glass is half empty or half full. Remind yourself that negative times pass just as positive ones do.

*

Taking action to invite positive change into our lives is almost impossible with a *bimbōshō* state of mind. We'll take a deeper look at fostering a greater sense of self-worth as we find out what drives us and how to follow our life's purpose when we discuss *ikigai* in Chapter I. But in the meantime, we can all stand to move out of our own way a little. Let's stop thinking with that poor man's mind, as we take Aimi Kojima's advice and learn more about seeking acceptance and balance. After all, if we're constantly worried about trivial things, we can't relax or be generous to others.

Chōwa 調和
Balance and harmony

Cats are known for always landing on their feet, and rarely do we see these graceful beings wobble. But is it possible for even the most elegant of creatures to lose their balance? The Japanese term *chōwa* translates into English as 'harmony', but in practice *chōwa* is much more than that. It is the quest for balance in an ever-changing environment.

The Japanese have a phrase, *neko no kangoi*, which roughly means 'a cat's craving for cold'. It suggests that even a cat, which usually craves sunshine, will eventually hide from the scorching sun. To practice *chōwa* is to pursue the most balanced outcome, and in it achieve a more harmonious lifestyle. Although sitting in the sun all day might sound like a good idea at the time, you're more likely to find greater success and contentment from a life that mixes leisurely pleasures with readiness and awareness.

After all, even the most lethargic cat is usually prepared for the sound of a scuttling mouse. Although their appearance can be calm, their senses remain attuned to the shifting patterns of the atmosphere, and with that they can confidently navigate any of life's challenges, without losing sight of what really matters most – lazing in the sun.

Shinto, Tao, and Zen Buddhism

If you've ever visited Japan, you would have noticed the general lack of aggression and outward belligerence you might find in some other places. Of course, that's not to say it doesn't exist, but it's most certainly less widespread and obvious. The politeness of the people who live there eloquently demonstrates a peaceful coexistence, and the poised felines of the country proudly share in this harmony.

Many cultural origins contribute to Japanese people (and their cats) living harmoniously, including *tatémaé*. This refers to the opinions aired in public often being different from what people really think. Not showing the world your true feelings creates a facade, especially in the workplace, that helps to maintain peace. But if taken too far it may err towards the negative Japanese idiom *neko wo kaburu*, which means 'to put a cat on one's head' – to disguise your true personality by pretending to be something you're not.

In addition to these cultural practices, the country is also interesting in that it has two main religions, Buddhism and Shinto, which cohabit peacefully. Unlike many other places, where religion can often be the cause of longstanding historical disputes and ongoing conflict, Japan remains largely free of religious tensions.

It's worth noting that these days religious practices aren't as common, and many younger people will tell you they don't subscribe to one particular religion in the same way their ancestors did, but peaceful cooperation still remains strongly intact.

Shinto's reverence for nature, balance, harmony, purity, family and ancestors has become so deeply embedded in Japanese society over the centuries that it is the foundation of much of Japanese culture. Shinto is the indigenous polytheistic religion of Japan, while Buddhism was introduced in the sixth century.

Zen Buddhism traces its origins to India, but it was in China that Taoism and Buddhism merged to form what we call Zen today. It's said that 'they formed a natural alliance which gave birth to the Ch'an School of Buddhism, later known as Zen in Japan'. Cat fan and famed scholar D.T. Suzuki, who is credited with spreading Zen Buddhism to the West during the twentieth century, described Ch'an (and Zen) as a 'natural evolution of Buddhism under Taoist conditions', and in his book *The Training of the Zen Buddhist Monk*, he warns that 'Modern life seems to recede further and further away from nature, and closely connected with this fact we seem to be losing the feeling of reverence towards nature.'

Like all evolving countries around the world, Japan's major cities are not immune from the global march towards modernisation and technological advances, which have undeniably brought about more convenience, but are also partly to blame for our mournful imbalance with and severance from the natural world. Despite these advances, however, Japanese culture is deeply rooted in ancient traditions that hold significant connections to the natural world thanks to Shintoism, Taoism and Buddhism. It's a place where you'll likely see temples and tower blocks sandwiched together, and where kimono-clad kids take photos beside the 18-metre-tall Giant Gundam Robot.

In-yō: the yin and yang symbol

Perhaps one of the most recognisable symbols of balance is yin and yang, known as *in-yō* in Japan, and also the Tai Chi elsewhere in the world. It's said to represent the universe as a circle, inside which two colours co-exist, together yet separate. According to Taoism, or *dōkyō* as it's known in Japan, the equilibrium of the universe is maintained by the yin and yang, which together contain all the opposing forces in the cosmos.

In general, things related to dynamic energy released outwards are yang, while things related to quiet energy kept inward are yin. Traditionally, yin is female, passive and dark, while yang is male, active and light. Other examples are listed below.

Yin	Yang
Stillness	Movement
Moon	Sun
Soft	Hard
Water	Fire
Winter	Summer
Night	Day
Earth	Sky
Plant	Animal
Female	Male

Compared with the outgoing characteristics of our canine friends, cats appear far more yin in their approach to life. Rarely do they seek permission to do anything, they do little to please others, and they don't seek approval – because they already know they're the best. That said, however, it's worth reiterating the importance of striving for balance. Even as far back as the ninth century,

Emperor Uda of Japan is said to have documented his beloved cat's behaviour in a diary indicating the feline's perfect balance between the two states. In the diary, Uda speaks to his cat: 'You also have a yin-and-yang mind and body like me. You do understand my mind, don't you?' Instead of assigning specific qualities to our personalities, we could all strive for a seamless shift between the two sides of this ancient philosophy.

Balancing ourselves

Sometimes we can feel like we're running against the wind, and other times we get the sense that it's propelling us forward. It's difficult to always know exactly what has happened – what we did right and what we did wrong. Life can end up feeling like a fickle hand, extending nurturing relief in one moment and a swift slap with the next. But maybe life isn't to blame. Perhaps instead we've just lost our balance and need to find some of that harmony that comes naturally to a cat. Could you be focusing more on work than your health, or on a lover more than your career? When we direct all our energy into one thing it can leave us out of whack, feeling physically tired and emotionally overwhelmed. When we work out what it is that is causing this imbalance it's important to take conscious steps to rectify this and prioritise ourselves. Yet, in today's super busy, yang-focused world, putting ourselves first can be a challenge.

Looking after yourself physically can be as simple as no-frills nutrient-dense meals, basic movement exercises, low stress and a healthy, cat-like attitude towards ample sleep. But just because something is simple doesn't make it easy.

On the subject of maintaining balance, Japanese Australian yoga teacher Yuri Bush suggests, 'Wherever you are, take a moment to breathe deeply, connect to yourself and see how you feel inside. Accept it and be kind to yourself and others. Practise this every day, you will find harmony.' Since the word 'yoga' means union, it can offer us a way of uniting the mind and body, and yin and yang, allowing us to create the space to begin nurturing this intrinsic connection.

Self-care isn't limited to yoga or sitting silently in mediation for long periods, it's as individual as you are. We all have the power to make choices, and when we choose ourselves as a cat would, it can help us realise our full potential and grow as individuals. When we take control of our decisions and do what's right for us in the moment, we will feel more empowered, worthy of life, and better able to turn our dreams into reality.

Balancing our schedules

The way cats communicate has evolved over time, but for humans the change has been much faster and more far-reaching, affecting not just how we live but also how we work. Never before have we been so connected and constantly reachable by friends, family and employers, but what does this mean for us?

Being reachable at all hours and having our peace interrupted is par for the course these days, yet it can leave us feeling like we never have enough time to fit everything in. If we don't make enough time for ourselves, work stress can manifest itself in different ways, from snapping at our partner to nagging neck pain. We all experience it at times, but the best things come to us when we accept these physical warning signs as a catalyst for change. These signals may be telling us that we are overdoing it and that we need to take steps to unwind, decompress and regain our cat-like balance.

Reading the signs your body gives you and slowing down at the right time can be the antidote to this fast-paced life. Restoring a work–life balance is integral to our ability to continue and avoid becoming burnt out. As Akemi Tanaka in her book *The Power of Chōwa* explains, the *chō* of *chōwa* can mean not only "'search" and "study", but also "preparation"'. In other words, in order to achieve a good work–life balance we need to take steps to prepare our daily schedules so as to not become overwhelmed. These steps will be different for everyone. Since it can be a fine balancing act to juggle what we have to do with what we'd like to do, avoiding burnout, or worse, *karōshi* (the Japanese term for death from overwork) by scheduling some much-needed downtime is vital for our mental health. Just as cats have set patterns for food, play, exercise and sleep, designating time for the things that bring us joy will help us thrive. One of my favourite Italian sayings is *Dolce far niente*, which means 'the sweetness of doing nothing'. This is something we will learn more about when we look at stillness in Chapter S. For the moment, though, consider how much time you spend doing nothing. If you could prioritise doing less for a while in order to achieve more balance in your life, what would that look like for you?

Incidentally, according to findings by the Organisation for Economic Co-operation and Development (OECD), Italians enjoy the best work–life balance in the world. This may come as no great surprise given that pleasant relaxation is so widely valued there that they even have a phrase for it.

Creating sufficient boundaries and creating enough me-time is integral to achieving balance. Whether you choose to do nothing in that spare time or to take up aikido is ultimately your call, but it's important to view rest and leisure as a necessary component of your well-being. If we spend too much time at work, we put too much emphasis on one area of our life and neglect the rest – the things that feed and nurture us. It's vital to plan time for these too, otherwise we risk losing sight of what's important. As the founder of philosophical Taoism, Lao Tzu, once said, 'Doing nothing is better than being busy doing nothing.'

*

The next time you're multitasking on your computer, doing what needs to be done in this yang-dominated world where striving often comes at the cost of stillness and non-doing, think of cats and how calm they are. Compared with us, with our endless notifications, to-do lists and digital updates, our feline friends seem to luxuriate in their own silence. If we are ever to achieve a more balanced life, we need to start making more time for ourselves, thus maintaining balance and preventing ourselves from becoming overwhelmed. As the famous saying from tenth-century Zen master Yunmen Wenyan goes, 'If you walk, just walk. If you sit, just sit; but whatever you do, don't wobble.'

Datsuzoku 脱俗
Break from routine

Although cats are generally creatures of habit, they still understand the benefits of breaking the boundaries and diverting from normal practice. If you have a feline friend, you may have noticed that their curiosity occasionally gets the better of them and leads them astray in search of a more preferable food source.

Datsuzoku is one of the Seven Aesthetic Principles of *wabi-sabi*, which stem from the practice of Zen Buddhism. Its original meaning is to be detached from all attachments, and unaffected by mundane affairs. From this we can surmise that by breaking with our usual routine, we will fully discover individual creativity and understand who we truly are.

While our daily habits can make us feel safe, they can also hinder our full potential. As the Japanese proverb goes, 'The frog in the well knows nothing of the sea', meaning we should be aware of the limitations of our own experience and knowledge. By venturing further than your perceived comfort zone, you will gain a new purr-spective on life. This can lead to greater opportunities – some of which you might have previously thought impossible. Why eat at the same place every night, a cat might think, when your neighbours might be holding something seriously scrumptious in their cupboards?

Sometimes, to regain that childlike wonder we once had, we have to expand our world by doing something that might at first feel uncomfortable. Ask yourself, when was the last time you did something for the first time? Sadly, too many of us have become slaves to our time-tables, so entrenched in smashing goals that there's barely any time to discover fresh paths. Travel is one way to open up new worlds that help us regain our curiosity, where we can marvel at our own enthusiasm for embracing new things, whether it's a new language, new culture or new cuisine.

But too often we tell ourselves there's more import-ant stuff to be getting on with, only allowing time for a small holiday or break once a year, which isn't enough to take more than a few tiny steps beyond the limits of our comfort zone. When given the chance to try something new, we may find ourselves saying no. This can inadvertently hinder our chances of experiencing something totally out of the ordinary. It can be good to ask ourselves why we say 'no' to new things, and to start thinking twice about refusing invitations. Scrutinise your reason for doing so. Are you really busy? Or are you just afraid?

To break free from our self-imposed barriers and restrictive routines doesn't always come naturally. Sometimes it can feel as though the house might burn down if we ignore our emails for one day, or as if diverting our calls could cost us our livelihood, but it's unlikely that any of these fears will become a reality. The benefits of shaking up the norm and doing something new may actually outweigh any assumed costs in the long run.

Escaping the ordinary

By transcending the conventional, we open ourselves up to a bigger world and see it with fresh eyes. Yet we can fear feeling overwhelmed and out of place, 'like a borrowed cat', as the Japanese say, if we dive in too quickly. You know yourself better than anyone, so if you want to open yourself up to a wider world but are anxious about doing so, do it on your own terms and take small steps that suit you. There is always something to be learned from new experiences, no matter how big or small they are.

Japanese artist Chie Tokuyama says, 'I strongly believe that changing my environment made my eccentric creativity even stronger and triggered a deeper understanding of life rather than continuing with routine work and a stable life.'

So how can we find the courage to escape the ordinary? When we start focusing on the exciting possibilities that lay ahead of us rather than digging our claws in against potential change, we may find that many more surprises appear, like all those new people we'll meet, the food we'll sample and the opportunities that await us. We needn't be filled with the anxiety of leaving home or starting afresh and not knowing anyone. Sometimes it's easier to repeat our steps in the forest than to make new ones, but if we never deliberately veer off course, we might not discover the sheer magic of surprise that awaits us. Taking those first steps beyond the safety and familiarity of the known into the unknown can open up new worlds of possibility, but too often we get stuck in our usual routines and don't allow for fresh adventures.

Letting go of labels

Let go or be dragged.

– Zen quote

Being freed from our usual environment also means being freed from the labels that define us. Can you imagine a cat bothering what other cats think about it or not taking the leap and doing what it wants? Why not drop all the negative baggage you may be carrying with you, and give yourself the opportunity to reinvent yourself? It's a lot healthier than staying static and dragging around a bagful of labels. Removing the harmful labels we inadvertently collect as we journey through life is a powerful and transformative way to re-energise ourselves and expand our horizons. As someone once said to me, 'by removing the labels you learn who you really are.'

Changing the way we think won't happen overnight, but it is key to our personal growth and development. We don't have to leave everything behind and start again on the other side of the world in an attempt to rebrand ourselves, but there is a level of work in finding out who we really are. Sometimes, detaching from harmful labels can mean cutting ties with dysfunctional patterns or separating from those toxic elements that could potentially be dragging us down. It might be a difficult path to walk, but it's worth the journey. Just as the traditional Japanese garden can surprise us at almost every turn, so can life if we allow it.

Letting go of past resentments

While being unbound by convention can free us, being unbound by our previous hang-ups can alter our future. Like a cat that latches on to a lizard, our attachments to past events can have an unhealthy grip over us if we don't try to let them go. If we see our previous unhappy experiences as valuable lessons rather than something awful that happened to us, we can change our perspective and our path.

Sometimes we can look outwards and blame our difficulties in life on others. Obviously, some things are not our fault, but if we continue to focus on them too much and use them to define our perspectives, we may never be able to move past them and may miss whatever auspicious changes come our way. No matter what we have been through, it's up to us to change the narrative and let go of those negative emotions that are imprisoning us. Without change from within, we only hinder our true potential and limit our possibility for transformative progress.

In his book *Letting Go: The Pathway of Surrender*, Dr David R. Hawkins, an author, psychiatrist, spiritual teacher and researcher of consciousness, explains that we have three ways of handling feelings: suppression, expression and escape. Suppression and repression are the methods we most frequently use to deal with our emotions, which can usually lead to projection and blame. The expression of feelings may free us from our negative feelings but it can give them more weight and leave others feeling like they are being dumped on or worse, attacked. The third response, escape, could come in the form of drink or drugs to avoid confronting our feelings. Escapism, if overdone, can lead to damaging effects and, in some instances, addiction.

Just as the sun completes its cycle, reaching its peak during the summer solstice and letting go, we need to accept what has passed in order to invite in the new. The challenge can be standing still for long enough and abandoning the desire for constant distractions in life.

The late Zen master Thich Nhat Hanh said, 'Letting go takes a lot of courage sometimes. But once you let go, happiness comes very quickly. You won't have to go around searching for it.' In the same way the Japanese cast away all of the past year's magic charms and Daruma dolls at temples or shrines in the New Year, perhaps we can shift our focus to something new by releasing our old attachments and belongings. We don't have to put elaborate decorations of pine, bamboo and plum (*kadomatsu*) outside our doorway as is customary in Japan, but we can let go of the unwanted thoughts in our mind that are holding us back.

*

Cats don't harbour negative thoughts and are not overburdened by labels; they live simply in the moment and don't care about the past or future. In the words of cat behaviourist and TV host Jackson Galaxy, 'Cats have nine lives, but humans only have one.' So don't spend it holding on to what's happened; release it, try something new, and see the magic happen.

E

Enryo 遠慮
Reserved attitudes

Place a hearty meaty meal in front of a dog and inevitably they will lick the bowl clean, often before it even touches the ground. But cats tend to show a little more self-restraint. Even when faced with a tasty bowl of tempting tuna, they continue to be able to demonstrate patience and poise, whereas an untrained pup would most likely have created a big mess on the floor. In Japan, this virtue of self-restraint is called *enryo*. A central tenet of Japanese culture, *enryo* encourages people to work together to prevent conflict through their own self-control. It prioritises the needs of the many over the individual, and encourages taking a pause before indulging a reactionary impulse.

But how exactly does this practice of *enryo* benefit our own lives? Let's consider an example: you're out on the main street, busy as a bee and desperate for a snack, so you pick something up as you walk. You could a) stuff your face as you walk, dappling your clothing in an abstract Pollock-esque work of art, or b) wait until you're sitting still somewhere and then enjoy your food.

As tempting as option a sounds, a little self-restraint here could pay dividends. Not only will you save yourself the time of cleaning your clothes, but you'll probably enjoy your food more. Taking the time to wait until a more appropriate moment to eat can give you the space to feel calmer, allowing you to connect with the act of eating rather than just stuffing your face. It could help you to make better food choices, be aware of when you're truly hungry, and prevent mindless munching.

While the original meaning of *enryo* is usually associated with showing reserved attitudes when others are close (often someone you don't know well, or who is older or higher in status), this example demonstrates how being considerate can benefit not just yourself but those around you.

Simple acts of self-control have the potential to impact your life in lots of significant ways. *Enryo* could help stabilise your mood, improve your interactions with others, and give you a better sense of overall calm. *Enryo* is a way of creating harmonious relationships with others by withholding your true wishes or opinions. But like most things in life, it requires balance. Performing *enryo* too much and constantly putting others before yourself is not good for your mood or mental health.

So next time you're out dining with friends and only one slice of pizza remains, wait before stabbing your hand into the centre of the table, and take some time to consider your next move.

Putting other people's comfort first is something many of us are rarely taught growing up, and offering the last slice of cake to a friend can be almost unthinkable, but these small selfless acts can make everyone's life more enjoyable, including your own.

Having empathy for others, thinking of the greater good, and not always putting yourself first are attributes that are undeniably beneficial to any individual or group, and that without a doubt contribute to a more cohesive society. There are many positive aspects to this characteristically Japanese concept. For one, a reduced tendency to be reactive and say whatever comes into our mind without considering the consequences can minimise tensions within relationships. Additionally, putting ourselves in another person's shoes gives us a different perspective, a new take on things that could look very different from what we've been telling ourselves. Doing things in haste or as a reaction to something rarely has any benefits. By factoring in the bigger picture and being mindful of others instead of only focusing on ourselves, we might actually achieve more calm in our lives.

Reading the air

There are various theories about the origins of this typically Japanese mindset. Some point to the country's religious roots while others to the origins of rice cultivation.

The Japanese concept *ba no kūki wo yomu*, which translates as 'reading the air', means sensing another's feelings. Historian and author Toyoyuki Sabata says of Japanese society, 'Harmony in the work environment is strongly stressed, and there is little self-assertion on the part of the individual.' He goes on to explain that this psychology and behaviour of the Japanese is thought to be based upon the traditions of rice cultivation, such as the fact that rice cannot be grown year-round, and the scarcity of suitable farmlands, coupled with the gratitude to one's ancestors for what land one has.

Composure and patience are key strategies in most sports. Yasuhiro Iijima, who worked for Japan Rugby Football Union for many years, explains more about *enryo*: 'Japanese culture is not individualism but groupism. Harmony is stressed in a group, where people who have a strong sense of individuality are considered undesirable. The approach of holding back is therefore a better way to make teamwork go smoothly. However, the young are gradually deciding that this way of thinking is old-fashioned and insisting instead on their own preference.'

Bearing in mind that a cat's sensory abilities are very acute, they are far better equipped to read the air than we are. A cat's whiskers can sense vibrations in the air, and it's said that they act like a sort of radar. Check the position of a cat's whiskers and see what they tell you. Dr Yuki Hattori, Japan's leading cat vet, says, 'Cats use their vibrissae [whiskers] for feeling things and touch is just as important as hearing for them.' Do cats have the ability to read the air? When a cat lovingly lays a gentle paw across its owner's face when the owner is sad, could they be performing *ba no kūki wo yomu*, and understanding the situation without words?

Yet the opposite would be true if they were to selfishly devour the last tasty pink prawn off their human's plate without their approval instead of waiting to share it with them. Then the cat could be displaying behaviour that might be described as KY – a derogatory Japanese slang term that stands for *kūki ga yomenai*, meaning they cannot read the air.

Being able to read situations without the need for explanations or requests is a level of thoughtfulness that is widely evident in Japan, from the gracious courtesy of *omotenashi* (hospitality) to the more personal experience of someone you barely know leaving flowers outside your door when they learn your beloved cat has passed away.

Reading the air needn't be a grand affair. It could be the more usual everyday scenario of opening a door for another without them asking or putting an umbrella over someone's head to keep them dry. Whatever it may be, this concept of being aware and conscious of someone else's feelings, offering kindness and sensing what another person needs without being asked, can generate a type of thoughtfulness that contributes to a more harmonious state of being.

*

Performing selfless acts out of consideration for others and holding back your own desires out of respect for another person's feelings is deeply entrenched in Japanese culture, and it's something we can all learn from. As the Buddhist saying goes, 'If you light a lamp for somebody, it will also brighten your path.'

Fukinsei 不均斉
Letting go of concepts

Often, when we are encouraged to think 'outside the box', we are meant to cogitate in an original or creative way. But what does this actually mean? Does it mean exploring ideas that are not limited or controlled by rules or traditions, or something more? Perhaps it's a new way of thinking that challenges our fixed view of the world.

Our feline friends don't consider what's in or outside of the box, they just look at the box. Maybe they see a flimsy cardboard cradle ripe for pouncing in, or a neat scratching post to tear up their frustrations. Either way, a cat will rarely consider whether the box is a perfect cube made of untouched Perspex, or a spoiled carton with rips and chips. Instead, they take the box for what it is, and admire its many possible functionalities for creative play.

Fukinsei is the second of the Seven Aesthetic Principles of *wabi-sabi* that we will consider in Chapter K, and encourages us to contemplate that the beauty and wonder we experience in the world is perfectly imperfect, not flawlessly curated. Like a playful kitten besotted by the joy of a tatty old box, we might think of our cats as purr-fect balls of fluff, but equally, pedigree breeders or cat show aficionados might think your mottled moggie to be a little less than the cat's meow. So the question is, does a less favourable appearance make something any less special? Or is this variation of characteristics and condition exactly why these things are so special? A tabby might not have a perfect 'M' marking on their forehead, or their tongue might hang awkwardly from the side of their mouth, or their nose might not be quite squishy enough for Instagram fame. But surely, it's these individual quirks that create beauty and uniqueness – just ask any designer.

Orie Kawamura, from 365cat.art, is a Japanese illustrator with over twenty years' experience. Her work captures the realistic nature of cats and can be seen on the covers of books and in textile design. Orie says, 'People can learn about freedom by observing cats,' and explains, '*Fukinsei* can mean beauty without the pursuit of perfection.' When she uses it in her artwork, she says, 'It's a type of distortion of the image.'

Theories of aesthetics fall within the study of Zen philosophy and of other disciplines concerned with how we place superficial value on what we purr-ceive. According to positive psychologist Tim Lomas, 'In Zen, art is seen as a particularly potent way of communicating spiritual truths, indeed, far more so than discursive prose.'

While most cats know the difference between a dish of organic chicken and a can of Whiskas, they tend not to care about how the packet looks, or how we present their dish to them. To appreciate something for its individual qualities, however aesthetically flawed it may appear at first glance, is a virtue many of us could stand to improve. That could be relishing in a messy meal for its nutritional density or taking a moment to admire the intricate differences in the asymmetrical markings that make one kitten cuter than another. Described as a central tenet of the Zen aesthetic, the idea of controlling balance in a composition via irregularity and asymmetry is embedded in *fukinsei*.

The natural world is brimming with examples of tragic beauty, from the fleeting impermanence of the cherry blossom in spring to the overgrown charm of a neglected garden or the intensity of a volcanic eruption. *Fukinsei* highlights that the natural world, like us, is not in perfect symmetry, but is instead intricately and often imperceptibly imbalanced.

How we see the world can certainly impact how we experience it. Have you ever noticed that sometimes we only see what we want to see or hear what we want to hear? Like the times when you have overheard a conversation and got the wrong end of the stick only to learn later that you made most of it up in your head. It's difficult to know if our feline friends can appreciate aesthetics the way we do, since they don't see colour or form in the same way, but rarely do we see them pursuing perfection. Instead we see them enjoying the moment and not wasting time judging others. So perhaps they are naturally more Zen in their way of being without even trying.

Kintsugi: Repairing with gold

The art of repairing cracks with molten gold, fixing a once unusable item and turning it into a valuable piece is known as *kintsugi*. While it is unclear when exactly this practice began, it is commonly thought to have become popular in Japan in the late fifteenth or sixteenth century. Author Kelly Richman-Abdou says the method treats the 'breakage and repair as part of the history of an object, rather than something to disguise'. Applying this principle to people, maybe we can also cover up our cracks and create a masterpiece.

If we were to allow ourselves to move away from perfection and instead embrace the things that make us unique, we could let go of the concepts that might be holding us back. Our imperfect laughter lines tell a story and show the wisdom we have acquired. Should we not be happy we have lived to tell these tales rather than lament the disappearance of our younger selves? Can we see our flaws as growth rather than the cracks in a living wreck? Of course that's easier said than done, especially if you live in a Western culture so obsessed with youth. If we can embrace our irregularity instead of running from it, however, we can perhaps live more peacefully.

When applied to tangible human experiences, *kintsugi* can encourage us to 'wear our scars' without feeling the need to hide them from the world. Systematically styling your life like a perfectly curated Instagram page is tempting, but it only produces a disingenuous representation of who you really are. Your defects and defeats, your flaws and your failures, every stumble and snafu helped you grow and made you the person you are today. These are the very parts of you that you should celebrate the most.

Perhaps, if you can learn to love your life's pitfalls as much as your achievements, and view them as the wounds of a masterful warrior instead of trying to discard them in shame, you may find that your misadventures are marvellous mini-lessons or that your flops and slip-ups provide you with fruitful insights. By reframing your thinking in this way, you can continue to grow and develop not just from your accomplishments but your failures as well.

The Zen circle: the *ensō*

The *ensō* is a painted black circle that is often an incomplete shape and is said to symbolise a range of things, from the circle of life and letting go of expectations to the beauty in imperfection. Drawn with only one brushstroke, it is commonly seen in Japanese calligraphy and is thought to represent our innermost self at its most authentic. According to Zen Buddhism, in the act of drawing an *ensō* we expose our true self completely.

Engaging in Japanese calligraphy, including drawing an *ensō*, is a practice that allows us to quieten the mind. To appreciate the beauty of the brushstrokes and understand the concept of creating something beautiful in the moment, without being able to modify it in the future, is a beautiful concept. *Fukinsei* is a reminder to be a denier of perfection. The idea suggests that by balancing irregularity and asymmetry, we can create a composition that captures something truly unique and perfectly imperfect.

*

Zen Buddhism suggests that nothing is perfect, lasts forever or is ever completed, a concept known in Japan as *mujō*. This word means that nothing is permanent, that life is transient and constantly changing. *Fukinsei* enables us to understand the benefits of seeing the beauty in impermanence and of being able to move beyond a fixed perception of the world – just as cats do.

Ganbaru 頑張る
Doing one's best

The commonly heard Japanese word *ganbaru* means to try your best, keep at it and never give up. The continuing effort to overcome obstacles is an important concept in the Land of the Rising Sun, and the number of words and phrases that reflect this is extensive. The word *ganbaru* is often used as a term of encouragement, especially when a task is particularly challenging or unpleasant.

An excellent example is the Japanese sleuth cats that kept sneaking into the Onomichi City Museum of Art for years. No matter how many times these kitties were ejected, they continued to demonstrate unwavering tenacity until finally, one day, they were allowed inside.

Or you could imagine the challenges involved in training a cat to walk happily on a leash. There might be times you would just want to give up and go back inside, but if your aim was to get out and experience the world with your feline sidekick, it would be important you finish the task. No matter how many times your cat wriggled out of their harness, if you embraced the teachings of *ganbaru* and kept at it, one day it would all just click.

The verb, *ganbaru*, according to Yasutaka Sai in his book *The Eight Core Values of the Japanese Businessman*, 'implies exerting great energy or emotional vehemence, thought, or action to accomplish an objective, particularly in the face of adversity'. Much like the Brave Blossoms as they fought to honour Japan in the 2019 Rugby World Cup against the high-ranking South African team. Or a cat in its endless pursuit of play, never giving up the chance to jump on the red light of a laser toy, so diligently watching the small crimson spot as it darts back and forth across the floor. Such effort is commendable. It's very rare to find a cat that will concede defeat, even if it has become momentarily immobilised by a slipped collar wrapped around its front legs.

So why is this concept helpful? I believe that it's the way we react to things in life that can have the biggest impact on us. If we falter at every hardship, how can we ever succeed? Transforming adversity into something that not only challenges us but also benefits us can seem impossible when we're facing obstacles. Still, if we take a step back and consider the permanency of our pain, and ask ourselves how long it will actually last and how it might benefit us in the long term, we may find the strength to push on despite the hindrances, and discover something meaningful that could make us stronger. Instead of trying to push our problems away and even run from them, we could look at them as an opportunity for transformation through being creative rather than reactive. Since most of us are at the mercy of our own minds and grasp onto negative thoughts easily, we have a tendency to dwell more on difficulties than obtainable objectives. It's been reported that around 80 per cent of the thoughts we have are negative, so is it any wonder we often give up before we've even started?

What if we didn't get caught up in these negative thoughts? The way we deal with and view life's challenges will impact our quality of life, from creating bad sleep and dietary habits to bouts of anxiety and depression. Whether or not we sit and dwell on negative thoughts and allow them to colour our future can make all the difference. Cats don't worry about all that life throws at them or fixate on how to control each setback. Instead they focus on the things that bring them joy, such as basking in a small beam of luscious sunshine or indulging in a long grooming session. Trying to concentrate on the things we can change rather than those that are out of our control will ease much of the stress in our lives. While *ganbaru* teaches us to carry on and be resilient, we also ought to know which challenges are worth tackling.

Despite the usefulness behind the concept of *ganbaru*, we also need to be cautious when applying it, as no one should have to experience *gaman* – suffering in silence. If used carelessly, *ganbaru* could appear insensitive to those on the receiving end. You may want to consider its appropriateness if talking to someone who is experiencing a serious situation such as illness or grief.

Fall down seven times, stand up eight

The Japanese proverb *Nana korobi, ya oki*, which translates as 'Fall down seven times, stand up eight', means choosing never to give up hope, no matter what life throws at us. Life doesn't always turn out how we want it to, and it's a natural reaction to give in to fear and anger, throw our hands in the air and ask why me?

It's important to remind ourselves that everything is constantly changing, and that even our darkest days will eventually pass, just as our good ones do. If we think like this we can begin to feel less weighed down. Everything in life is impermanent, nothing stays the same. The Japanese are said to resort often to the idea of *mujō* (impermanence or transience) in order to alleviate their feelings of sadness about death. While most 'Westerners [seek] beauty in "eternal beings", many Japanese have a strong tendency to seek beauty in transforming things'. Kenkō Yoshida, a Japanese monk, writing in the fourteenth century, once said: 'The most precious thing in life is its uncertainty.' For many of us, this concept will be completely alien and difficult to adopt, but being aware of the fact that even the most difficult times can in hindsight be seen as a gift, can lessen our overwhelming sensations in the present so that we may keep moving forward.

To slog on tenaciously through tough times is a very Japanese concept and somewhat similar to the 'Keep Calm and Carry On' poster produced by the British government in preparation for World War II to raise the morale of the public. This type of stoicism embodies the need to remain calm in adversity and dig deep in times of strife. To build this kind of inner fortitude takes courage but also the ability to cultivate patience, recognise the moments we get angry, and try to change our response. It won't happen overnight, but if you start small and keep building your awareness, in time you'll notice you are able to let go of the things that once triggered you. Eventually we may develop the equanimity of a cat and always land on our feet.

The boy who drew cats
Let's consider another essential characteristic of the *ganbaru* spirit, perseverance. In the story *Neko wo egaita*

shōnen, a popular Japanese fairy tale translated by Lafcadio Hearn, we hear about a boy who has an insatiable desire to draw cats. This compulsion becomes so severe that his parents send him off to become a priest, but even the priests can't tolerate his incessant cat drawings and expel him from the temple. Feeling too ashamed to return home, the boy finds another temple, takes out his brush and stubbornly draws more cats. Unbeknown to the boy, the temple has been possessed by a rat goblin. After he falls asleep, a great fight ensues, and when he wakes, he realises he didn't just draw any old cats, but cats that could slay rat goblins. He was alive because he drew cats. He listened to himself and kept drawing cats. Eventually, when the villagers heard his story, he became a hero.

The main character learns that following your heart's desire and never giving up on what you believe in is the only way to survive. The story illustrates how sticking to your guns and not being swayed by others can eventuate in something positive. Too often we give up because it all seems too hard, or we get side-tracked by others' thoughts and beliefs. But if we fully commit ourselves and stay on our chosen path, never giving up no matter how many bumps in the road we face, our perseverance will ultimately pay off. Like a cat trying to pinch a prawn off a plate, achieving goals comes through diligence and determination, not through avoidance and disbelief.

Task

Before going to bed each night, write your experiences of the day and divide them into what has been positive, negative or neutral. By keeping us mindful of our daily experiences and drawing our focus from our negative thoughts (remember, about 80 per cent of them are inclined to be pessimistic), this exercise can help us embody the *ganbaru* spirit. You may be surprised by what you see and then choose to use your energy to focus on something different.

Positive	Negative	Neutral

*

It's important to remember that everything has a lifespan, even the most challenging of times, so it's always worth taking the time to lick our wounds and get back on track. If we remember to look at our difficulties as temporary rather than permanent, we can find it a lot easier to deal with the negative feelings associated with them and keep going until we cross to the other side. With a little *ganbaru* spirit, you will find the strength to do your best even in times of adversity.

Hara hachi bu 腹八分
'Eighty per cent is perfect!'

It's generally agreed among scientists that cats can't taste sweet things since they lack the receptors for it, and that cakes and other sugary items are of no interest to them. Unlike us, they don't salivate at the sight of a chocolate éclair or strawberry ice cream, so they have a head start on us when it comes to healthy living. For humans, though, the alluring temptation of a sweet treat is difficult to ignore. As the list of foods we're supposed to eliminate seems to grow each year, so does the number of fad diets. But what if achieving a healthy lifestyle was less about following a specific diet and more about reducing mindless overconsumption?

The term *hara hachi bu* means 'Eat until you're 80 per cent full'. This concept goes much further than just food though, and can be used to negotiate the trappings of purr-fectionism. It's said to have originated in the book on Zen Buddhism titled *Zazen Yōjinki: Notes on What to be Aware of in Zazen*, which recommends eating two-thirds as much as you might want to. *Zazen Yōjinki* is an introductory and instructional book on *zazen*, a Buddhism meditation practice, written for beginners by author Jōkin Keizan, who lived from 1268 to 1325.

While this concept might seem outlandish to those who like nothing more than gorging themselves at all-you-can-eat buffets, allowing their desire for food to overtake any self-control, it's a simple and effective way to increase our health and life expectancy.

Smaller paw-tions

Although most cats prefer smaller portions, it's been said that dogs, like some humans, show little restraint when it comes to eating – chowing down on every last morsel, practically eating until they explode. In contrast, very few cats will eat until they are ready to vomit all over the floor. Instead, they politely leave a few remnants in the bowl for you to clean up.

That said, recent research by leading Japanese vets suggests that, surprisingly, even feline waistlines are beginning to bulge. According to one report, in Japan, approximately 56 per cent of cats have been diagnosed as obese or overweight.

Obesity is a serious issue today for animals and humans alike, and is considered a modern epidemic across most of the globe. It's reported that 890 million people around the world are living with obesity, and childhood obesity is expected to increase by 60 per cent over the next decade, reaching 250 million by 2030.

While Japan has largely avoided the obesity crisis, that's not to say it doesn't exist. It is, however, a remarkably smaller problem than in other countries, with only about 3.5 per cent of the population classified as obese compared to rates in the United States and elsewhere of 30 per cent or more.

Of course, it's not just how much we eat, but also what we consume as well as the amount of regular activity we get. Many Japanese cats live inside tiny city centre apartments with little space to run around, are quite likely to be indoor cats, and are often fed a diet of highly processed food. Their inactivity and diet will be a contributing factor not only to tremendous weight gain, but also their mood.

While it can be difficult to change our relationship with food, the long-term benefits, such as increased life expectancy and a reduced risk of developing chronic diseases, are difficult to ignore, both for ourselves and our pets.

My friend Hiroko Shimada, a gemstone merchant

from Takayama, says, 'If you eat too much, it strains your whole system – not just your stomach but everything. You use up all your enzymes to digest food.' Hiroko and her ninety-year-old mother, Miyori-san, regularly ferment their own food, and experiment with creating concoctions like mustard leaf pickles to ensure they are consuming enough naturally fermented produce. Hiroko goes on to say, 'Although many Japanese are still conscious of *hara hachi bu*, the Western notion of large portions being good value for money has gradually become more popular these days.'

The Japanese proverb 'Eight parts of a full stomach sustain the man; the other two sustain the doctor' may suggest why there have been so many centenarians in Japan, particularly in Okinawa. Unfortunately, research suggests that nowadays more than one in two Okinawans are obese due to the influence of the Western-style diet or junk food!

Many studies have been done on these so-called Blue Zones, which include the islands of Okinawa in Japan; Sardinia in Italy; the Nicoya Peninsula in Costa Rica; Ikaria in Greece; and Loma Linda in California. The healthy habits of the Blue Zone inhabitants are widely debated, and many people believe the longevity of the centenarians in these areas is mostly down to a lack of stress and a more communal lifestyle.

It is still possible, however, to assume some of the healthy habits exhibited in Blue Zones, even if you don't live in the same country or have exposure to the culture? Simply by cutting out unhealthy processed foods, eating only when you're hungry, reducing stress, contributing to your community, and increasing your exercise, you could begin to experience life in a different way.

Something as easy as slowing down your eating can also have a significant impact on health. A Japanese study of type 2 diabetics has shown that by 'simply chewing longer and pausing between bites [we can] prevent obesity and lower health risks like diabetes in the long run'.

In an undomesticated habitat, where food is not widely available, cats would naturally eat several small meals a day. Research has shown that even if a domesticated feline has access to food, they will split their intake over different feeding sessions. Vets therefore advise this approach as the most beneficial to a cat's welfare. Long before the arrival of supermarkets and Uber Eats, when we humans were hunter-gatherers, we would eat when we could, and our portion sizes would often have been far smaller due to food scarcity or how skilled we were at hunting and gathering. The ability to order highly palatable, ultra-processed food 24/7 makes over-consumption easier, and makes it more difficult to stop when we're only 80 per cent full.

If you've ever been to Japan, or to a Japanese restaurant, one thing you'll notice is the size of the plates. In a typical Japanese eatery, not only will the dishes be aesthetically pleasing but the plates will also very likely be palm-sized, whether you're dining at a sushi train or an *izakaya* (inn). These smaller dishes allow people to try various types of food, in a similar way to tapas, and also act as a type of portion control, which can curb the desire to overindulge. Depending on how much you order, and whether or not you clean your plate, of course.

Macrobiotics: a yin and yang approach to food

In the 1920s, long before Madonna espoused the benefits of a Japanese macrobiotic diet, George Ohsawa, the founder of macrobiotics, believed that in order to be healthy we should follow a simple diet, consume meals in moderation, and live in greater harmony with nature. The principles of his diet included reducing animal products and eating locally grown, seasonal foods. In 1960, Ohsawa published *Zen Macrobiotics*, and four years later the first macrobiotic cookbook, *Zen Cookery*, which has been updated and revised numerous times since. According to George Ohsawa, too much yin or yang in our food can lead to imbalances in our body. It's interesting to see his list of which foods he considered more yin or more yang. Foods with a high yin are said to be 'cooling foods', including (but not limited to) apples, cauliflower, chickpeas, kale, mushrooms and soybeans. High yang foods, on the other hand, are considered 'warming foods', and include such things as beef, caffeine, chicken, eggs and fried foods, as well as alcohol.

Mayumi Nishimura, who worked as Madonna's private macrobiotic chef for seven years, says, 'By selecting foods and cooking methods that harmonise with the natural cycle of energy, I can help my clients – and myself – achieve a healthy body and a tranquil mind.' Mayumi, who was born in Aichi prefecture, Japan, moved to the United States as an adult and trained at the macrobiotic Kushi Institute in Massachusetts before writing several books on the diet.

Nowadays, with rates of obesity increasing, it is worth researching different styles of eating. Even your moggies might enjoy switching from a pre-packaged diet to a more natural one, perhaps with a macrobiotic intake of steamed pumpkin and organic chicken.

Avoiding purr-fectionism

The *hara hachi bu* ideal doesn't just relate to food but also other activities, such as your work. How many times have you been told that something needs to be perfect before you can show it to others, or that your portfolio must be 'just so' before you send it out? This type of advice could make even the most talented people miss opportunities in their pursuit of perfection. If you wait for perfection, that moment of opportunity could pass you by like a bus on a rainy day.

Even people in the business world can see the benefits of working smarter and leaving a margin of imperfection. Inspired by the Italian economist Vilfredo Pareto, the Pareto principle or 80/20 rule was developed by Joseph M. Juran and is a time-management technique with the idea that 20 per cent of actions are responsible for 80 per cent of outcomes.

In her book, *The 1 Day Refund*, productivity coach Donna McGeorge says, 'Aiming to perform at 85 per cent not only takes the pressure off; it allows you to play the game for longer, giving you an advantage over others.' This creates space for you to recharge and be at your best the next time you're in the office.

The Japanese word *kodawari* means the 'relentless pursuit of perfection' and is something to be admired in those with an uncompromising quest to be the best. Think of the country's great traditional craftsmen or the famed sushi chef Jiro Ono, who take such pride in their work. While we are unlikely in reality ever to achieve perfection, we can still take great care in what we do and take pride in our work. Is a cat that spends time grooming itself trying to achieve a perfect appearance or simply looking after its glossy coat?

The modern idea of perfection is often fuelled by what we see in magazines, on TV and on social media. It has become common for us not to accept ourselves as ordinary, but instead want to be seen as successful, wealthy and glamorous. While it's fine to have these kinds of aspirations, it's also okay to allow ourselves to just be. As the Buddha is reported to have said, 'Success isn't the key to happiness. Happiness is the key to success.' In our constant striving for perfection, we run the risk of feeling like something is lacking from our lives, and of ignoring all the good things by placing too much emphasis on what we don't have instead of what we do. Ask yourself, do you really need a bigger house, a bigger car or a better job to be happy? Sometimes it's good to refocus the lens and centre on the positive things we already have in our life, such as our health, family, friends and pets, rather than constantly reaching for external desires we think will make us happy.

The endless need to strive and compete can lead to unhappiness. Life passes us by so quickly, it doesn't make sense to be wishing for a more perfect version of ourselves in the future – it's the here and now that are important. After all, when you finally get to where you've been dreaming of, you may feel let down and disappointed. In the words of the American novelist Gertrude Stein, 'Whenever you get there, there is no there there.'

The notion of 80 per cent being the new perfect can be applied to many other aspects of life. It can teach us to pay attention to everything we're consuming and how we're spending our time, offering another valuable lesson in self-restraint and how to avoid overindulgence (see Chapter E: *Enryo*).

How to practice *hara hachi bu*

Ask yourself the following questions:

1. When was the last time I was eating, felt satisfied and stopped when I was almost full?
2. What size plates do I use? (Try using smaller dishes when you serve your next meal.)
3. How do I eat my food? Do I chew enough? (Practise eating slower, counting how many times you chew each mouthful. Thirty-two times is the suggested amount . . .)
4. Am I eating without paying attention? For example, do I eat my food at my desk or while I'm on the phone?
5. What do I need to be truly happy? What are my core values?
6. What changes do I need to make in my life to stay true to these values?

Where *enryo* focuses on self-control for the greater good by considering the needs of others before our own, *hara hachi bu* teaches us the benefits of self-control from a personal perspective. Learning to be more intuitive and mindful of the way we interact with people, and of what or when we consume – not just food, but also things like entertainment and the news – can have a big impact on our life.

How many times have you stayed up late to watch an extra episode of your favourite TV show only to wake up the next day feeling groggy and wishing you hadn't?

Can you imagine a cat missing out on its sleep to do something so fleeting?

The restraint that results from paying attention and fighting the urge to overindulge can help us in myriad ways. It's worth remembering that just because something feels good doesn't mean you should do it all the time.

Ikigai 生き甲斐
Life purpose

If you haven't heard of it before, you'd be forgiven for thinking *ikigai* was some kind of exotic sushi or a particularly venomous species of jellyfish. But in fact *iki* means 'life' and *gai* means 'worth', and when combined, these words mean 'something that gives your life purpose'. Much has been written about this Japanese concept in recent years, and about the dramatic impact that finding your own life's purr-pose can have – giving you a reason to leap out of bed each morning with vigour, like a hungry cat. While some people are fortunate enough to know what they want to be from an early age, it might take a while for others to recognise their dream.

Let's begin this chapter by looking at some examples of *ikigai* in action.

In the snow-capped city of Takayama in the Japanese Alps, you'll find plenty of small local businesses that were started out of a passion for something. Unlike the faceless franchises taking over the high streets in the Western world, replacing smaller family-owned companies, there are still many businesses in Japan that offer something unique. One such example was the bar Desolation Row, which was dedicated to the music of Bob Dylan. Thoughtfully decorated, the one-roomed bar with Dylan memorabilia adorning the walls was hugely popular with locals and tourists alike, and the late owner Kensei Mori would often 'forget' to charge his punters at the end of the night, so great was his love for what he did. Then there's Heianraku, a simple family-run restaurant owned by Hiroshi Furuta and his wife, Naoko. This restaurant manages to top the TripAdvisor rankings for the area – no mean feat for a tiny eatery based in the Japanese Alps. So what is it these two places have in common? Their passion and character, and their owner's love for what they do sets them apart from other businesses and makes them so well liked.

Behind the success of these unique businesses are no intricately designed slogans, aggressive sales targets or dedicated marketing team. What differentiates them from your average bar or eatery is authenticity, which seems to be lacking in many places nowadays. Both places have a great vibe that makes people feel instantly connected and draws in customers from all over the world. Neither business is particularly driven by the need to be the best, make bucketloads of cash or achieve rapid growth, but their popularity seems effortless.

Japanese author and scientist Ken Mogi writes, 'It is true that having *ikigai* can result in success, but success is not a requisite condition for having *ikigai*. It is open to every one of us.' In other words, this democratic concept doesn't require you to have a degree from a fancy university or come from a privileged background; all you need is a passion for what you do.

In fact, *ikigai* doesn't need to be connected to your work or making money. It can just be something that motivates you. Take the rockabilly dancers of Yoyogi Park, Tokyo, who spend most weekends gyrating to 1950s rock'n'roll. This subculture dance group, which gathers at the Harajuku entrance to the park to perform, has become popular with tourists over the years. As you get closer, you'll hear the fractured music coming from a boombox and swarms of people circling around to inspect the spectacle closely. Some will be gawping, others taking photos. Like a Nipponised version of the musical *Grease*, rockabillies of various ages strut their stuff to mostly 50s numbers but will occasionally let loose to a more random tune like the 1980s song 'Boys Go Crazy', the music roaring out from beefed-up speakers on the pavement. In Japan, there are no strict rules around sticking to a genre, especially if that genre is from outside the country. It's great to see how dedicated they are and know that they dressed as 1950s greasers in their black leather biker jackets and tight black jeans with no other purpose than to get together, dance and enjoy themselves. Then, there were the Irish cosplay musicians I witnessed in an Irish pub located in an innocuous building in Osaka. Surrounded by a cornucopia of Celtic memorabilia, the duo was playing traditional Irish folk music and appeared to be as Irish as leprechauns, with their green waistcoats and linen flat caps. Everything about them screamed 'Emerald Isle' just a little too loudly, from the clothes they wore to the instruments they played, but on closer inspection, the flutist was as Japanese as J-Pop. The performers clearly enjoyed playing to the crowd, and their total immersion in another culture.

Similarly, the owner behind the YouTube-famous cardboard-box-loving feline Maru is unlikely to have foreseen his immense fame and fortune as one of the most viewed cats on the internet before they posted the first 'I love a box' video. The clips went on to launch the Japanese cat's career as a celebrity kitty; he once held the Guinness World Record for the most YouTube video views of an individual animal. It all started from a love for Maru and a joy in observing Maru, and finally evolved into a passion for curating images and videos of the cute kitty's antics to share that love and joy around the world. Then, there's Maro, the adorable tabby 'cat-grammer', whose owner, Rie Matsui, dresses Maro up in homemade costumes and poses him in front of seasonal dishes and world cuisine. Maro, who is currently managed by a well-known agency, embodies his owner's passion for food, photography and cats.

So how do you find your passion if you don't know where to start? It can be as simple as concentrating on your strengths and the things you like, or opening yourself up to new activities that you'd never even considered. Taking small steps to find out what you are passionate about is all part of the fun of being alive. For example, you might like to travel but have never thought about writing down your adventures, or you might know you enjoy dance but have yet to even touch upon the myriad different styles out there.

You needn't break the bank by going to expensive workshops or classes to find out what you like. There are hundreds of everyday opportunities for you to meet like-minded people and explore new avenues of interest. You could volunteer at a local organisation whose values align with your own, say yes more often to your friends' offbeat invitations, or head to the library and soak up as much new knowledge as you can. Putting yourself into new situations and building upon existing hobbies are both great ways to jump-start your journey to discovering who you are, and to ignite your passion, whatever that may be.

Finding your purr-pose

Putting your passion into practice can be a transformative experience. Whether you pursue it as a career is up to you. For some people, trying to monetise it could ruin their love of doing something that makes them happy. For others, getting paid for what they love might seem like an impossibility. Taking the time to get to know yourself and what really gives your life meaning can help you uncover your true potential. Part of this is learning to believe in yourself and your abilities, as well as staying true to your individual motivations by avoiding negative, external influences and not being bound by societal pressures or preconceptions about what it means to find success.

Discovering your *ikigai* can help you achieve balance in life and focus on the positive. When times are tough, having that one thing that gives your life meaning can help you pull through the darkest moments. Viktor Frankl was an Austrian Holocaust survivor, neurologist, psychiatrist, philosopher and writer whose theories were heavily influenced by his suffering in the concentration camps during World War II. Frankl was the founder of logotherapy, similar to *ikigai*, a theory that focuses on the importance of finding meaning in life through having a purpose. Frankl said:

The way in which a man accepts his fate and all the suffering it entails, the way in which he takes up his cross, gives him ample opportunity – even under the most difficult circumstances – to add a deeper meaning to his life.

Unless you are extremely fortunate, finding your *ikigai* won't happen overnight, so it's essential to take small, dedicated steps to carve out where you want to be. Being a part of an environment where you feel comfortable is key, and can help you discover what you're most suited to. Since we are often influenced by what our friends and family think, we need to bear in mind that we are all unique and have our own path to follow. There's little benefit in getting caught up in other people's dreams if they don't match our own.

Follow your passion

Job satisfaction is something most people desire but find hard to achieve. Few of us are fortunate enough to make money doing what we love. Since *ikigai* is often considered the fine balance of combining these two things, let's look at someone who has done this successfully.

Yukari Satō was born in Kauai, Hawaii, to a Japanese mum and French dad. Since childhood, she's lived all over the world, working in the financial industry in Tokyo, Hong Kong, Singapore and more recently London, where she currently lives with her partner and Muffin, a rescue cat Yukari adopted from the UAE. Unlike most people who work in banking, Yukari was never a money-driven person and decided to change her career to one that she was truly passionate about. In 2016, when she received permanent residency in the UK, and after much consideration and budgeting, she took a risk, quit her successful banking job, attended Le Cordon Bleu culinary school for a year to train as a chef, and has worked in restaurants, hotels and cafe kitchens since 2017.

Yukari says, 'I've always had a passion for food, both eating, and cooking and baking. I would often spend all day Sunday in the kitchen and make packed lunches for the week to take to the office, and baked goods to share with the team on Mondays. I love everything about cooking, from browsing cookbooks to menu planning, going to grocery stores, and the actual process. I would often finish a long day at work, come home, and spend an hour or so chopping vegetables to turn into soup. I found the process relaxing and therapeutic.'

It's clear that Yukari knew food was her passion yet pursued a very different career in banking first. It can be difficult to know which path to take, especially when we are young, but if we embrace the journey of real-world experiences, over time we can discover what really makes us tick.

Yukari says, 'Food was *ikigai* for me throughout my life. I'm definitely in the camp of "live to eat" rather than "eat to live". Knowing I could have a nice breakfast was what got me up in the morning. I would always look forward to lunchtime, even in kindergarten and still to this day, and I also love cooking for others. I feel *ikigai* knowing I'm able to cook for family and friends; it is something I look forward to all the time. It keeps me relaxed, healthy and balanced.'

After observing her cat, Muffin, Yukari has concluded that felines also have their own version of *ikigai*. She explains: 'They'll have favourite spots for their various activities and one of their *ikigai*s may just be keeping a watchful eye on what they can see from the window. Muffin loves to watch the foxes, squirrels, birds and other cats, and also the leaves falling, raindrops, and is curious about everything. Their days are filled with doing what they love.'

Yukari adds, 'Although I earn much less now, and all jobs have an element of stress, I certainly feel more *ikigai* every day.'

Feline the flow

We've all heard the phrase 'go with the flow', which for me conjures up an image of a docile Birman being carried around in a backpack. Feeling no need to escape or scratch at its owner, the fluffy feline is just happy to go with the flow. But the flow associated with *ikigai* is less to do with lazily permitting the passing of time, and more to do with finding those moments when you're doing things with the utmost focus and joy. Award-winning artist Minuella Chapman describes it like this:

'When I'm working in my studio on my art, it becomes a timeless experience. I lose all sense of time.'

As mentioned earlier, our feline friends have the ability to be in the moment whether they are chasing a laser toy, climbing trees or watching birds. It's the type of focus we give to something that we truly value and want to immerse ourselves in. For artists and writers, getting lost in the visual imagery of a painting or in the words on a page are examples of flow. When you experience flow, you never clock-watch. Psychologist Mihaly Csikszent-mihalyi, who recognised and named the concept of 'flow', describes it as 'the state in which people are so involved in an activity that nothing else seems to matter; the experience is so enjoyable that people will continue to do it even at great cost, for the sheer sake of doing it'.

Whether cats have their own version of *ikigai* is difficult to say, but they are very honest with themselves and listen to their bodies instinctively. They'll rise when they've had enough sleep and feel rested, demand food only when they're hungry, resist the urge to overindulge, and ask to play when they're feeling energetic enough to do so. They'll sleep when they're tired or feel under the weather, and cuddle when they want affection.

Paw-sized passions

The original meaning of *ikigai* isn't linked to money, but rather a curiosity to learn more about something, such as savouring the mellow grassy notes of a green tea and discovering where it came from, or growing your own vegetables. Talk of purpose in today's capitalist world has moved away from this original concept and has inevitably led to discussions about profiting from it. Who hasn't been bombarded by an influencer's feed yelling about how to cultivate profit from your hobby? But this is moving away from the original meaning of *ikigai*, and can lead to burnout. As with most things, balance and moderation are the key.

If you consider how cats break up their day, they don't have one ultimate goal they are constantly chasing. Instead, they have several meaningful pursuits, which play out over the course of the day, from getting up in the morning to going outside, climbing a tree, bothering some insects, tending to their fur, and slumbering in the afternoon. If we viewed our passions as things that give us pleasure rather than to be conquered, not only would we have more fun doing them, but the end result would be far more authentic.

Writing in 1943, psychologist Abraham Maslow proposed a pyramid-shaped hierarchy of needs to describe human motivations. At the top is self-actualisation. Like us, cats will need to meet all their daily requirements such as food and water before seeking feelings of accomplishment. If we set our end goal too high, it could become unreachable, causing us to fall from the tree we've been climbing and leading to more pain and anguish.

Having paw-sized passions to attend to over a designated time period can leave us more fulfilled and less likely to feel disappointed when things don't go our way. This idea seems to be a return to living in the moment and enjoying the doing rather than the end goal.

Cats perhaps demonstrate this best by their approach to catching their prey. It can take time, and often turns out to be a fruitless endeavour, but rather than becoming impatient, they wait it out patiently in a shady patch, enjoying the breeze ruffling their fur. Even when this pursuit is ineffective, a cat can try again the next day without feeling disheartened. This is because cats love to hunt, almost as if it's their life's purpose. Of course, for wild cats, hunting is an essential activity, undertaken purely for survival. But even within the well-fed household moggie rests something primal and instinctual, a link to something they were born to do, an urge to pounce fiercely upon the red dot of a laser pointer, without becoming stressed that there really is nothing there to catch.

Although scientists use various ways to measure cats' hunting success rates, and the outcome can be affected by variables such as whether their habitat is open, research suggests that even lions are only successful in about 20 per cent of their hunts when working individually or 30 per cent when working as a group. The most successful feline hunter is the black-footed cat (*Felis nigripes*) native to South Africa, Namibia and

Botswana, but it achieves no more than 60 per cent success. According to one Australian study, domestic cats land around only 32 per cent of their prey in vegetated areas. This rate increases significantly in open areas. (And while this examination of hunting is useful for demonstrating a cat's purpose, we should not forget the destructive impact introduced cats can have on native wildlife.)

In life, there will always be things we're not keen on doing, but if we can break up our day with our paw-sized passions, it may alleviate boredom or annoyance. For a writer, a small passion could be as simple as picking out perfect stationery to take notes, while for a pet owner it might be choosing a new diamanté collar, or for a sculptor using different tactile materials. These small simple passions are unique to everyone – but that's the beauty of it.

Discover your purr-pose

Ask yourself the following questions:

1. What would I do without being paid?
2. What am I curious to learn more about?
3. What things make me want to get up each morning?
4. Have I ever experienced blissful concentration? When?
5. When was the last time I heard or saw something that made my eyes sparkle? What was it?

How do you know you have found your *ikigai*?

Finding something that gives your life meaning and puts a spring in your step is symptomatic of achieving it. You'll know when you have found your *ikigai* because the task you're undertaking will start becoming more immersive and difficult to walk away from. Individual passion, however, is not something we are readily taught in school or by our parents. Rather, it is something deeply personal and often evolved over a lifetime of experiences. For this reason, it requires you to listen to your inner voice, and uncover the things that make you tick. But trying to figure out what you love while hoping it will make you a boatload of money could take you round in circles. It could change something beautiful into an endlessly hungry monster that continually needs feeding. Instead, your passion should be something unconnected to the purpose of making money and tied only to enriching your soul. Of course, if it results in a windfall of cash and allows you to live comfortably, then that's an added bonus. But ultimately the goal should be to find something that gives you verve and vitality. A reason to be.

Jōshiki 常識
Common sense

It's accepted practice for a cat to stalk a mouse, slowly, purposefully, before quickly pouncing on its prey. Although independent and sometimes seemingly wild by nature, cats prefer the safe predictability of things done in a certain manner, and dislike the instability of not having a set routine. This is why a common set of rituals done in a particular way helps them thrive. A cat will react when their litter tray is moved to a new location, or their usual feeding time is altered. Or imagine cat-sitting for a friend, and in a moment of innocent ignorance, you use an unfamiliar feeding bowl instead of the one the cat feels accustomed to. How might they respond? It's very likely the cat will look at you accusingly with a stare that could be translated to 'How do you not know that? It's common practice.'

The tricky thing is, of course, how to know what correct behaviour is when you haven't been previously informed. Common knowledge in these instances is instinctive for the familiar cat owner, but these rituals and practices will have been formed locally, within the confines of the cat's home, creating a standard of principles that will help maintain harmony for those who live there.

The Japanese word *jōshiki* was originally created as a translation of the English word 'common sense'. But many Japanese people often use the word to refer to social norms or manners. For native English speakers, the idea of 'common sense' is generally something that is objectively logical, such as not swimming where there are sharks feeding or avoiding stepping out in front of a bus. Common sense in this instance is a cross-cultural set of life skills that help to keep us alive. Yet in Japan, the type of common sense for which we use the word *jōshiki* could also include cultural concepts that dictate the way things should be done so that everyone is on the same wavelength. It could be a learned skill, a ritual, etiquette or honouring cultural conventions. In this way, *jōshiki* helps to keep society running smoothly and prevents unnecessary complications. It's probably easier for us to think of it as common cultural knowledge than what we would usually call common sense, otherwise it could lead to one of those 'lost in translation' moments.

Nolico Suzuki, a Japanese educator, describes *jōshiki* as having two main meanings. The first is common knowledge. 'For example, don't you know that the Japanese don't eat ramen with a fork but with chopsticks? That's *jōshiki*.' The second meaning has more to do with etiquette or good manners: 'It's *jōshiki* to not call others after ten o'clock [at night], or play with your chopsticks during a meal. Lastly, if someone smokes without asking others, he has no *jōshiki*.'

Looking at the wider context, educating yourself about proper customs and cultural 'common sense' generally makes it easier to navigate unfamiliar situations. For example – while cat-sitting for a friend you don't know so well, you could avoid some trouble by simply knowing the particular customs of that household. Or when visiting a country you haven't been to before, you can thrive by gaining a better understanding of what might be expected of you, or what could be considered offensive behaviour. But this concept runs much deeper than simply avoiding being considered deviant or disturbing your neighbour's cat with the wrong bowl. By becoming more skilful in certain situations, like preparing for an exam by familiarising yourself with the subject matter, or understanding the rules before you play a game of chess, you are acquiring common knowledge, and giving yourself a better shot at success. Through adapting to new and unknown environments and ways of doing things, you not only widen your perspective but also become more flexible.

Cats that live with humans are said to have learned that meowing is the best method of gaining our attention, and even change their sleeping patterns to fit in with their owner's timetable. They are also extremely adaptable and good at surviving in different types of environments, from travelling around the world on ships to surviving in a wide range of climates. They are successful because they are flexible and can change to suit their new habitat.

Jōshiki in Japanese culture

Although some notions of 'common sense' around the world may be the same, such as not sticking your hand in a fire or walking out in front of a speeding car, there are some that are unique to Japan, and for the average *gaijin* (or foreigner) can be a minefield when trying to negotiate the rules of Japanese social etiquette. Your strange behaviour will show you up as an outsider if you don't exercise the assumed logic that everyone else uses. As Sue Shinomiya and Brian Szepkouski write in their book, *Business Passport to Japan*:

> Ignore protocol in Japan at your own peril. Deeply embedded in the Japanese psyche is a sense of the way things ought to be done. Japanese common sense, or

jōshiki, means knowing that there is only one right way to do something.

There are even some situations where *jōshiki* could lead to public persecution for a minor transgression, such as putting out the wrong garbage bag on the wrong day. This will most likely result in a large yellow label being stuck on the offending bag for the world to see, so that everyone knows the person who put it out lacks *jōshiki*, resulting in public shaming of the worst kind.

Yet at its core, *jōshiki* is there to serve the people, and keep order, so that everyone is on the same page. Relying on these rituals and practices helps to unify and bring a sense of security. Let's take a look at some more examples of *jōshiki* concerned with typical Japanese customs.

Finders aren't always keepers

Japan is exceedingly good at returning lost property. William Park and Johanna Airth said: 'In 2018, more than 545,000 ID cards were returned to their owners by Tokyo Metropolitan Police – 73 per cent of the total number of lost IDs. Likewise, 130,000 mobile phones (83 per cent) and 240,000 wallets (65 per cent) found their way back. Often these items were returned the same day.' Wouldn't it be nice if when you misplaced something, it was returned no matter how big or small it was? When something gets lost in Japan, it is likely to be handed in to the police station without hesitation. The Japanese rarely break the rules, and honesty is highly valued. Author Brian Bocking says honesty, or *shōjiki*, plays a crucial role in the Japanese moral character and could be related to the 'Buddhist notions of karma and individual moral accountability'.

British rapper, singer, songwriter and Japanese enthusiast AJ Tracey tells a story from his time in Japan that perfectly illuminates this attitude. While he was shooting the video for his song 'Buster Cannon', he went into A Bathing Ape store, spent a ton of money, then forgot all about it, leaving his shiny new garments on a bridge. When he returned two hours later, some kind soul was humbly waiting alongside the bags, hoping to return them safely to their rightful owner. Tracey said, 'No one would do that in London.'

It's been well documented that after the tragic events of the 2011 Tōhoku earthquake and tsunami, very little looting occurred, which many media outlets suggest was surprising given that it's usually common practice during a state of emergency. Yet accounts of looting seemed virtually non-existent in Japan. Theories on the reasons why vary, such as police presence, the enforcing order of the Yakuza, the universal altruistic response to others in times of need, or simply the Japanese people perfectly demonstrating their *jōshiki*.

Showing gratitude

Similar to *Bon appétit* in French, or a little like saying grace, in Japan people say *Itadakimasu* before eating. In Japanese culture, people say thanks, not just to the cook, but to nature, and the animals and plants that sustain us as well. *Itadakimasu* means 'I humbly receive', and expresses an appreciation for many things people in the West often take for granted. Closely tied to the Zen Buddhist view of interconnectedness, it displays an awareness not only of our connection to other people but to the air we breathe, the soil, and the plants and animals that feed and nurture us.

Wouldn't it be nice to be thanked for your efforts when you leave the office every day? In the Japanese workplace, *Otsukaresama* or 'Thank you for your work' is a common phrase, used when you want to express gratitude among colleagues. Similarly, *Gokurosama deshita* is often used by bosses or superiors towards their subordinates. It's important to remember when responding to this to use *Otsukaresama desu*, and not *Gokurosama desu*, or else you could be seen as impolite and not knowing your place in the strict office hierarchy.

Hot-spring bath etiquette

*Onsen*s (or hot-spring baths) are an extremely important part of Japanese culture. If you are familiar with Japan, you might be au fait with the notion of *onsen*s, or even have had the pleasure of peacefully soaking away your troubles in the tranquil waters. For the average Westerner, however, the strict rules of conduct surrounding bathing are seldom recognised. The problem is that many Japanese automatically think other cultures should know what to do in a bathhouse and are often horrified when we don't. It's up to us, therefore, to find out how to perform the correct order of the *onsen*, because it's unlikely anyone will tell you to your face when you are fully naked in a bathhouse, knee-deep in sulfurous water, about to commit an atrocity in the steamy confines of a *shōji*-screened spa, because that would be considered impolite and shameful. If you're lucky there may be signs to instruct you, 'the outsider', not to make a complete fool of yourself. These are usually displayed in, you've guessed it, English, and demonstrate to the ignorant *gaijin* how to bathe and act properly. Here you can study what you could do wrong in any number of situations, from correct hair washing to proper towel use. For the Japanese, standing while taking a shower before using the spa is a major faux pas, as is shaving or using soap in the *onsen*, or even talking. To outsiders, these rules might seem strange, and a little strict, but they make sense within the culture. To avoid looking barbaric, it is advised to follow the rules carefully.

These common values are about more than just keeping yourself clean and not offending those around you.

The predictability of them makes people feel safe, and also acts as a significant tool in helping to maintain a polite and orderly society.

Gift-giving customs

Gift giving is another example of how things are done in a particular way in Japan.

Presentation is everything – the way a gift is wrapped is considered as important as what's inside. There are many traditions around gift giving in Japan. For example, when meeting up with someone, even people you see often, you always bring a little something to exchange. There's also the concept of *okaeshi*, or a return gift, which is fairly unique to Japanese culture, and involves buying a gift for someone who has given you one. The gift should cost around half the value of the original present.

An *omiyage* is a souvenir you bring back exclusively for others and not yourself. This gift is usually locally produced goods from the region you visit, and displays a kind of thoughtfulness to friends, colleagues or family when returning from your journey. It's said to date back to the Edo period, when only a few privileged pilgrims would go away and bring back gifts for those who were unable to go.

As with many cultures, there's always a 'thank you gift' given at celebrations, for example at weddings, funerals and births of babies.

The notion of giving thanks remains front and centre for the Japanese people, with several occasions dedicated to gift giving such as *ochūgen* in the summer and *oseibo* in the winter. These gifts are generally given by someone who would like to express gratitude and appreciation to a person. It's also customary to politely refuse your gift at least twice before accepting it. If you accept your gift the first time it is offered, you could be considered greedy.

Living more skilfully

Despite being highly adaptable, like us, cats are creatures of comfort and generally prefer to remain in their own homes. When confronted with the unfamiliar, their natural instinct is to hide away in order to protect themselves until such a time that they can feel confident within their new environment.

But no matter how wonderful it might feel to curl up in a ball on a nice warm spot of sunlight and laze away the days until they're all gone, at heart cats are born adventurers, eager to discover new feeding sources and scope out the neighbourhood. Rather than diving in full force and possibly ending up in an unfavourable situation with a more seasoned resident, the wise kitty bides its time, learns the lay of the land, and plays the game of life with prowess.

We shouldn't allow our own feelings of unease to impact others when life inevitably throws a new challenge our way. Embracing routines and customs helps things run more smoothly. Familiar activities are comforting during difficult and uncertain times, and help us when we feel unsettled. With that in mind, this quote from twentieth-century Zen monk Shunryū Suzuki highlights the value of the status quo: 'Zen is not some kind of excitement, but concentration on our usual everyday routine.' The Noble Eightfold Path, perhaps the most widely known Buddhist teaching, is valued as a practical guide on how to live our lives. The fourth stage, 'Right Action', suggests how to act skilfully without craving, selfish desire, hatred or ignorance.

Having a set of guiding principles can help us feel secure, which is why customs and common practices are beneficial and a part of human societies. Once we realise the importance of daily rituals and how they help us function, we will understand the need for personal limits in achieving harmony with others. Examples include limiting the need to speak loudly in public, embracing the chance to listen to other people's points of view (even if you disagree with them), and respecting other's beliefs and customs. Similarly, maintaining social etiquette, showing gratitude and having awareness may not only help to prevent feelings of isolation and anxiety but also bring us closer together.

*

Replacing our own personal rigidity with flexibility allows us to adapt to different circumstances – and opens us up to a new way of doing things. We don't just learn something about another culture or custom but also more about ourselves.

When cats live in social groups they also need to follow a common set of practices to avoid inter-cat aggression, such as not taking what's not theirs and respecting each other's space – even if they don't like each other. Even in uncertain times, wise kitties wouldn't trespass where they shouldn't, or be unappreciative of the hand that feeds them. These are all good *jōshiki* traits that make dealing with others less complicated and life a little more Zen.

K

Kanso & Kokō 簡素 枯高
Simplicity & Austerity

Do you know someone (perhaps you) whose cat's toybox is overspilling with unused toys? Perhaps Marie Kondo needs to sprinkle some 'spark joy' and simplify that home.

While the type of 'decluttering' Kondo is famous for is known in Japanese as *danshari*, which literally means 'cut, dispose and leave', incorporating *kanso* and *kokō* into your life offers simplicity and austerity, which can help you be more selective in what you buy and keep. These are the third and fourth of the Seven Japanese Aesthetic Principles we will consider. It's said that these seven pillars of *wabi-sabi* are found not only in nature, but also in the human character and behaviour – thus we could all benefit from reconnecting with them.

The seven principles to achieve a *wabi-sabi* way of life include:

Fukinsei – **Let go of concepts**
Kanso – **Simplicity**
Kokō – **Austerity**
Shizen – **Naturalness**
Yūgen – **Ethereal beauty**
Datsuzoku – **Break from routine**
Seijaku – **Tranquillity**

We looked at *datsuzoku* in Chapter D and *fukinsei* in Chapter F, so let's now consider the importance of *kanso* and *kokō*. *Kanso* allows us to find clarity of mind through the removal of non-essential clutter. By applying this to your daily life and deliberately forging clearer spaces, you can calm an overburdened mind, begin to feel more centred, and work more efficiently. *Kokō* is a way of thinking that sees beauty and value in old and ageing things, especially for their presence and strength emanating from within. In relation to *danshari* or 'cut, dispose leave' if you see beauty and value in old things, you don't have to keep buying new ones. Rooted in the Zen philosophy of *wabi-sabi*, these concepts incorporate living more minimally in order to gain inner peace, which in turn will make you feel lighter.

In previous chapters, we talked about how creating simple rituals in your daily life can help you to be not just more balanced and organised but also more productive. When applying the concept of *kanso* to your home or workspace, you construct a more pleasant environment in which to spend your time. If you have ever felt your life is empty despite it being filled with things and people, perhaps it's time to consider viewing things a little differently.

Surprisingly, the minimalist movement that's popular today stemmed from an art movement that started in 1960s New York, and has since produced an array of books, podcasts and blogs. Perhaps two of the best-known minimalist advocates in recent years are American authors, podcasters, filmmakers and public speakers known as the Minimalists, Joshua Fields Millburn and Ryan Nicodemus. They promote a less-is-more lifestyle, saying that a rich life has nothing to do with wealth and that we wrongly fill the void with consumer products and try to buy our way to happiness.

When we have too much stuff, it can be difficult to be organised and live stress free. In his book *Zen: The Art of Simple Living*, Buddhist priest Shunmyō Masuno says, 'happiness is not found by seeking out extraordinary experiences but by making small changes – to what you do, how you think, how you interact with others and how you appreciate the present moment.' To illustrate, the author highlights how simple methods such as lining up your shoes after taking them off can bring order to your life. For me, there's nothing more frustrating than the missing sock conundrum, especially when you're frantically rushing for an important appointment. While this sounds like a first-world problem, it's one that is easily avoided. You can remove the frenetic last-minute search if you match socks immediately after they've dried and throw out the odd single ones, saving you time and annoyance in your morning routine.

As a child, I was never one for tidying – my love of writing stories and drawing pictures of horses and cats trumped any inclination to clean up, which resulted in a muddled and messy desk, piles of papers peeking out of their respective drawers and clothes stacked upon each other. Years later, though, I have learned to appreciate the benefit of being able to find something when I most need it, thanks to bare benchtops and simple spaces. Kondo would be proud.

Cut, dispose, leave

Due to her huge success and popularity, Marie Kondo – or KonMari, as she's also known – is a Japanese organising consultant, author and TV presenter, and has even inspired feline-owning fans to create a hashtag dedicated to the famous KonMari Method. If you search #KonMariCats on Instagram, you'll see pictures of cats sitting in neatly organised drawers or on empty shelves.

A post from one user states: 'Nothing on these shelves was giving me joy.'

The method includes a range of ideas such as 'tidying by category' – not by location – beginning with clothes, then moving on to books, papers, *komono* (miscellaneous items) and, finally, sentimental items. 'Keep only those things that speak to the heart, and discard items that no longer spark joy.'

When applying this approach to favourite items that you've held onto for years – like a favourite top from ten years ago – you do start to question whether it is the item or what it represents that makes you cling to it so tightly. Perhaps, it brings back past memories of a fun night out with friends, a favourite sports team or an old boyfriend. Whatever it may be, could it be time to let it go, fold it neatly and say 'Thanks for letting me wear you', as Kondo would advise?

While Marie and her method might not be to everyone's taste, it's interesting to note that this concept of being grateful to an item for letting you wear it appears to be connected to the Shinto belief that items have a spirit or *kami*, which we will look at in more depth in the next chapter. For now, though, it's worth pondering whether we can truly live in the present if our homes are filled with things from our past.

Someone who has taken the Zen-inspired philosophy of *kanso* to the next level is the Japanese author of *Goodbye, Things*, Fumio Sasaki. He describes how, after living in the same apartment for ten years, he had accumulated so much stuff he felt as though he wasn't moving forward in life. He writes: 'I said goodbye to almost all my things and to my surprise, I found I had also changed myself in the process.'

It can be hard to let go of items that once brought us so much joy, but if we can turn our attention to the fact that they have been simply gathering dust in our cupboards or on top of our shelves, we may feel less resistance when we come to let them go, and more inclined to release them. Every time I've moved, I've realised how much superfluous stuff I have amassed, especially books. Although initially these were one thing I felt hesitant about releasing, I was happy to discover a Korean church that was collecting books to send to a charity in Nigeria. I felt then that my books would go on to give others enjoyment, and so I became less sad about saying goodbye to them.

It's worth noting here that while taking our unwanted items to a charity shop is a great way to dispose and discard, we should also be mindful that people don't want our rubbish, so only offer items that are in good condition. It's been widely reported that some countries have become dumping grounds for our waste, so don't give others items that are so worn that you would not use them yourself.

Shedding your belongings is never easy, but you can make it less painful to declutter, minimalise and invite in the new. One phrase that springs to mind is 'If you wore a trend the first time around, you don't get to wear it again'. Although this concept can feel uncomfortable at first, the benefit of applying it outweighs the drawbacks. Firstly, depending on our era, we really should have moved on from wearing army jackets and hipster jeans, but secondly, when we hang on to an item just on the off chance it might make a resurgence in the world of fashion, we're not really living in the present. If we eliminate what we no longer use, we create more space to invite in new possibilities. A good rule of thumb is to ask yourself, 'Have I used this item within the last year?' If the answer is no, then there's a good chance you don't need it anymore.

Are cats minimalists?

Despite some pet owners' best efforts to dress up their animals, cats remain the ultimate minimalists. They are the epitome of travelling light: they only need something to sleep on and bowls to eat from. As any cat owner will tell you, they are also the best declutterers. No surface is left untouched by those pesky paws and their penchant for pushing things off. As a result, many people who live with felines purposely remove from sight plant pots, photo frames or that precious vase your great-aunt Sylvie left in her will, for fear that they're going to crash to the floor and break. Even if you're not one for empty counters and sparse spaces, you'll no doubt notice how much easier they are to clean. It's hard to beat having nothing to pick up and clean under and no marks left on your wooden cabinet from years of having an assortment of ornaments gradually discolouring the wood.

I asked specialist cat gift shop owner Kumi Tonooka why people like to dress up their pets and whether she thinks cats are the best minimalists. She says, 'People want to show their pet's cuteness to other people and get likes on social media.' But when it comes to living simply Kumi adds, 'Cats only need food, water and their personal space. They don't need many possessions.' She suggests that people can live more simply like cats by 'trying not to be manipulated by advertising'.

But for the serious human minimalist, can pets be part of a minimalist lifestyle? It seems opinions vary on the topic, and while pets can be considered possessions by some, most animals are happy with just the basics and are therefore not going to overly burden you. If you are serious about living more simply, though, perhaps avoid buying your pet an unnecessary sweater or swanky bed, which are really just for your own amusement, and instead keep only what is functional.

We don't all need to be strict minimalists, but because it's admittedly fun to splash out once in a while, it's worth considering if you really need something before you buy it. How vital is it to your life? If you have ever saved for a designer top or an expensive car, you will no doubt have felt ecstatic about acquiring it at first, but then immediately become worried about damaging it. Sometimes we have to weigh up whether our possessions really bring us joy or simply add to our stress.

An uncluttered mind

You can also apply *kanso* and *kokō* to other parts of your life, such as how much input you experience each day. This input can come from social media, distractions from other people, and noise in general. We get to choose what we focus our minds on, so why not make better decisions that will benefit us in the long run, and aim to limit negative input?

Author and computer science professor Cal Newport, in his book *Digital Minimalism*, says that the usual recommendations such as turning off notifications or observing a digital sabbath are not sufficient. Instead, starting off with strategies like a 30-day 'digital declutter' could help you feel calmer and more in control. Finding the time to organise your digital world may seem extreme to some, because technology is meant for our convenience, right? But if you find you are feeling exhausted rather than energised by your devices, maybe it's time for a digital declutter. This might mean, for example, unsubscribing from cat blogs you know you're never going to read; or choosing which is your favourite photo of a sleeping kitten out of the 1000 virtually identical ones you took, having that one printed and then deleting the rest. There are so many ways we can reduce the time we spend staring at our screens.

In order to acquire a decluttered Zen mind, it's suggested that we reassess our priorities and the common belief that we need more to be happy. The way we measure success is often based on what we have and how many possessions we own rather than on what we've achieved. Author Robert W.F. Taylor uses Buddhist monks as an example of the benefits to be gained from freeing yourself of stuff. Their limitation on owning things as a way to free the mind and remain on their chosen path is an inspiration to declutter. Not only does the liberation from belongings allow fewer distractions and more focus, but it frees up time to spend on more meaningful pursuits.

Zen Buddhist master Shunryū Suzuki once said, 'If your mind is empty, it is always ready for anything. It is open to everything.' In other words, when our minds are full, we're unable to make space for anything new.

Whether your thoughts are optimistic or pessimistic, they still clutter your mind in the same way as the clothes in your wardrobe. It might be time to start thinking differently and use a variety of tools to start clearing away the excess noise. Declutter or organise your home, practise meditation as a tool to ease the mental chatter, and take the time to realign your values over to something more meaningful than just accumulating worldly possessions.

As we've seen, *kanso* and *kokō* not only encourage us

to live more simply, but also help us transform the way we live. If we dump the old, we can get to a calmer state, which beats being overloaded and cluttered like a hoarder with an oversupply of cats. Furthermore, by incorporating the Zen Buddhist teachings of non-attachment, self-discipline and simplicity, we can be less tied to our belongings, which in turn could allow us to feel a new sense of freedom. Like a magpie collecting shiny objects, or a dog burying bones all over the garden, excessively accumulating resources might help us feel safe and in control. While there's often no harm in buying the odd item here and there, having more things doesn't necessarily foster our long-term wellbeing.

Tips for living more simply

1. Avoid impulse buying – if you like an item, give it some thought; don't rush to buy it.

2. If unworn clothes have been in your wardrobe or closet for longer than a year, chances are you won't wear them again much in the future.

3. Discover a charity you like and find out if they have a shop for you to take your unwanted items to.

4. Perhaps make some cash out of your unused items, depending on their condition – ask around and see what you can find out.

5. Be mindful about why you're keeping something. Is it still relevant to your life today, or is it time to let it go?

*

Cats don't really feel the need to stockpile things. Although some felines are known to hoard items, it's less common and opinions vary on why they do it. Some say it's an outward expression of emotional problems, others that it mimics food gathering for kittens. Whatever the case may be, compared with us, our feline friends don't continuously acquire material possessions or endlessly accumulate stuff they don't need. Kitties are more content to lead a *kanso* lifestyle.

Mottainai 勿体無い
Regret over waste

Have you ever wondered about cats' environmental paw prints, or shuddered at how long kitty litter takes to biodegrade?

If you have a cat and the sight of piled-up tuna tins in the recycle bin has you squirming like the lizard the cat has just brought in, then your regret over this type of waste could be a demonstration of what the Japanese call *mottainai*. While throwing out your cat's old tatty toys is definitely considered *mottainai*, the term can refer to more than just regret over material possessions, such as a wasted opportunity.

Origins of *mottainai*

Similar to the English phrase 'Waste not, want not', *mottainai* reminds us to be mindful of frivolously wasting resources. It's said that its origins are rooted in Japan's two main religions, Shintoism and Buddhism.

While researching this chapter in July, I serendipitously came across Jun Tagami and his partner Masayo Kurimoto, the owners of Inner Nature, a Japanese sustainable lifestyle store. It just so happened to be when the global movement Plastic Free July was taking place. They were busy promoting a Japanese cotton laundry bag made from *sarashi*, a type of old-fashioned reusable cloth, as well as natural pet products made from hemp. I was lucky enough to get their attention long enough to discuss the different ways we can all try to live more sustainably, as well as pick their brains about the connection between *mottainai* and Japan's major religions.

Jun had this to say: 'There is a belief that gods or life dwells in small phenomena as well as large natural phenomena, such as Amaterasu, the sun goddess, and Tsukuyomi, the moon god. From this idea, nature is not something to be conquered, but to live in awe of and in symbiosis with. Everything that exists in nature is sacred, and should not be wasted; this leads to *mottainai*. Next, in Buddhism, are the concepts of *inga ōhō* or karma/reward, which you can think of as poetic justice or getting your just desserts; and also *engi*, which means everything is connected and which is related to the concept of *mottainai*. This brings about the idea that one's actions will one day come back to one's life, and since we believe that everything is connected, we can think that wasting is equivalent to wasting ourselves.'

Shinto, like other animistic worldviews, believes that nature is full of gods and that all living things are equal. These ideas have existed since ancient times. To illustrate, Jun describes the *Man'yōshū*, the oldest collection of Japanese *waka* (Classical Japanese) poetry, which includes passages that express the hearts of insects. He also mentions the *Sankashū*, a collection of poems by Saigyō, a poet–priest during the late Heian period (794–1185). Jun says, 'There is a song in the *Sankashū* that discusses how the sound of insects brings comfort and prevents sadness during the long autumn nights.'

When I asked Jun how we can be less wasteful in our daily life, he said, 'I think we need to feel the spirit of *arigatō*, or thankfulness, every day. The original meaning of the word *arigatō* is a rare occurrence. For example, when we take the food we eat every day for granted, we do not appreciate it, and as a result, we easily waste it. By considering that it is a rare occurrence every time we eat, we can feel more grateful, and this will lead us to cherish the food we eat, which is *mottainai*.'

To implement this into our routines, we can start by being grateful for where our food has come from, taking the time to appreciate the growers or the producers, the soil in which the crops have grown, and the animals and insects that fed the soil. We could try to be more selective with what we buy, to make sure nothing is wasted or left in a cupboard to grow mould. We can do simple things like planning our weekly shop, then ensuring that what we buy doesn't deviate too far from our list once we reach the aisles.

While this might sound unadventurous to some, it keeps costs down and, more importantly, prevents excessive waste. Ask yourself if you really need ten half-empty bottles of shampoo on your bathroom shelf. Do you really want to watch a bag of spinach wilt in the dark corners of your fridge? Or, if you have a cat, will your kitty mind one bit if you don't pick up an extra toy for them on the way home?

As we have learned in previous chapters the idea of interconnectedness is central to Zen Buddhism. If we are to feel gratitude, it is also important to be aware of this idea that everything is connected. Jun explains: 'Even for a grain of rice, many things are involved: the person who grows it, the person who brings it to you, the person who holds the seed, the weather that made it, your health so that you can eat it, and so on. When we think about this complex and interconnected relationship, our gratitude will naturally lead us to *mottainai*.'

When Japanese people say *itadakimasu* before they eat, they are expressing thanks for all the blessings they have received. Jun says, 'I think the idea of respecting all living things may have led to the idea that the act of eating is a way of receiving life and having it live with us.'

But *mottainai* isn't necessarily just related to food, as Jun points out: 'Before making the decision to throw away clothes, you should ask yourself why the clothes came to you, whether there are other situations in which the clothes can be used, whether the clothes can be used for other purposes, etc.' The act of throwing away clothes without receiving their original value or purpose is considered *mottainai*. In this case, *mottainai* is a way of thinking rooted in a sense of humble gratitude that the clothes are not something that we have acquired, but something that has been given to us from the great flow. However, some might connect this concept to *mottainai* having its roots in the lifestyle of the pre-industrial era when people were generally poorer, and the producers of things people used daily were more visible in the community; it's more about material conditions than spirituality.

When I asked Jun if he thinks cats are wasteful, he said, 'In Shinto, all living things have meaning and are equal in their existence, and in Buddhism there is the concept of *engi* – everything has a beginning, everything is connected. The idea that all existence arises from karma and therefore there is no such thing as its own nature, essence or substance. From this point of view, we believe that pets are beings to be respected just as we are, and that every encounter with a pet has meaning. Not only good memories, but even sad memories have meaning for us.' Jun adds, 'When I was in Japan, I had a cat at home. I have never had a cat since I came to Australia in 1995, but now that we are selling hemp pet products, I have been able to get involved with pets again. I believe that everything that happens has a meaning, and therefore should not be wasted.' Finally Jun adds, 'I don't remember which cartoon or literature it was, but I remembered that it said "Cats are philosophers". In fact, when I had a cat, I remember my family often talking about how cats pretend not to know much, but they really know what they're doing.'

A green cat, a princess, and the 3Rs

It may sound like the beginning of a fairy tale or an odd joke, but what do these things have in common? Unlikely as it seems, they all carry the message of environmental protection.

Only in Japan would you find an earless green cat as a representative for sustainability in fashion. The international store UNIQLO chose the much-loved character Doraeman to represent it as a Global Sustainability Ambassador. When they turned Japan's adored blue character from blue to green, they did so for a good cause. By initiating 'Doraemon Sustainability Mode', UNIQLO aims to create a brighter future for the world by presenting the brand's sustainability initiatives in fun, accessible ways.

Doraeman, if you're not familiar, is a fictional character in an eponymous Japanese manga and later anime series, who travels back in time to aid a boy named Nobita. Created by Fujiko F. Fujio, *Doraeman* is one of the best-selling manga series in history.

But it's not just anime cats that carry an environmental message. Japan also highlights environmental causes through anime films such as *Princess Mononoke*, a 1997 animated epic historical fantasy written and directed by Hayao Miyazaki and animated by Studio Ghibli. Although there are several complex narratives in the film, the main plot of the movie is a struggle between the gods of a forest and the humans who consume its resources.

In addition to fashion and film, there's the 3Rs – reduce, reuse, recycle – campaign, and various coloured bins that are used to educate the public on how to properly sort trash and recyclables. In most households, garbage is usually organised into as many as nine different categories, depending on the prefecture, which can be a bewildering experience if you are new to the country. The complex waste-collection schedule can leave you perplexed and can be a steep learning curve if you are an outsider. To instruct citizens, printed calendars display the different times and dates the recycling is to be collected; they also indicate a puzzling variety of actions required before disposal, such as pulling off labels and removing bottle tops.

Surprisingly, despite having such a sophisticated waste-management system, the country's consumption of single-use plastics remains one of the highest in the world. Think how many of those little fish-shaped soy sauce containers, or *shōyu-dai* (soy sauce snapper) as they are known in Japan, must be used there each day. There are also lots of unnecessary plastic coverings in supermarkets or on convenience food. Reasons for Japan's excessive use of single-use plastics range from long working hours and commutes, to the service culture and gift-wrapping to very high standards of hygiene. But as I'll demonstrate next, there is one small town with big ambitions when it comes to zero waste.

Kamikatsu: zero-waste town

Located on Shikoku, the smallest of Japan's major islands, you'll find Kamikatsu. Little known until fairly recently, this town has made international headlines with its mission to be Japan's zero-waste town. There's no waste collection service, so the locals have to cart all their waste to a central facility, where it is segregated into more than forty-five categories. I contacted Momona Otsuka, who is in charge of the centre, and she kindly provided me with information on the initiative. With a population of 1500, Kamikatsu was the first municipality in Japan to set itself the target of zero waste. As well as its central garbage facility it has a learning centre, thrift shop, public hall and hotel. Using the principle of the 3Rs, the locals separate their rubbish at the centre, leaving any compostable waste to be broken down at home. It's said that 80 per cent of their overall waste is recycled.

Kamikatsu is not the only zero-waste town globally, however. In fact, six other municipalities are developing ways to minimise plastic waste. These include Alaminos in the Philippines, Capannori in Italy, Pune in India, Flanders in Belgium and, in the United States, Austin and Seattle. These initiatives prove that with the spirit of *mottainai* it could be possible to make zero waste a reality anywhere in the world.

Regret over past or missed opportunities

While we can take actions to curb our use of single-use plastics and reduce our waste, there's not much we can do about the past. All we can do is change our response to it. If opportunities present themselves, it's up to us to be mindful not to waste them.

Another trap we can find ourselves in is overusing the words 'should' or 'if only'. It can be unhelpful to continually say things like 'If only I'd said that' . . . or 'I should have done this', since we can't undo what has already happened. But we can learn how to deal with it better in the present and endeavour to avoid it in the future. We need to recognise that there's a difference between our thoughts and our feelings. If we allow our thoughts to run rampant like a cat doing zoomies, we give them attention and energy that we could be spending on something more positive.

While it may be useful to feel remorse over a missed opportunity, since it shows recognition of our behaviour, it's unhelpful to get stuck on it and beat ourselves up. The danger is that we don't move beyond remorse – and remain static. The past is only beneficial if we're using it to better ourselves in the present. So the next time a door swings open, think twice about closing it too quickly, or else you could be wasting something valuable.

*

It's difficult to know whether our feline friends show regret about the past or not making the most of a given opportunity, since they seem to live mostly in the present. All we can try to do is be grateful for what we have, live more simply and not be wasteful – three things I'm sure you'll agree most moggies do naturally.

Natsukashii 懐かしい
Bittersweet nostalgia

Have you seen how the sound of the fridge door opening seems to trigger joyous moments in a cat's memory and send them leaping towards their food dish? Or how the sight of a lost toy from behind the couch creates pleasant recollections of past playtimes and plunges them into a heightened state of happy frolicking?

In a similar way to cats, we can find ourselves transported back to a particularly wonderful holiday by the scent of a certain sun cream, or feel locked in a moment from our youth as we hear the familiar beat of a particular song. For me, the burnt fragrance of *mitarashi dango*, or rice dumplings, will forever remind me of Japan.

The aroma of those skewered balls covered with a sweet soy sauce glaze as it wafts through the streets of Takayama characterises my treasured memories of my time there. These precious moments from our lives, the ones that are ingrained so deeply within our hearts and minds, are to be cherished.

Natsukashii is commonly used in Japan when experiencing something for the first time in a long time. The term is similar to what we call nostalgia, but its meaning is deeply intertwined with an appreciation for the events of the past, without feeling a need to grab hold of them from their place in time, but instead harnessing them as a lesson in being thankful for what once was. The Zen expression *Nichinichi kore kōjitsu*, which literally means 'To have a good, happy and peaceful day, day after day', teaches us that each day is an irreplaceable juncture in time that will never happen again. It refers to a mindset of living our lives with great care and attention in order to appreciate the importance of each passing moment.

Past memories can appear alluring in their dreamlike fantasy, tantalising us with powerful images of yesteryear and leaving us yearning for more. The trick, though, is not to hold on to them too tightly, but instead be grateful that they occurred at all. If we get too hung up on past stories, they can prevent transformation and change, so it is vital to practise self-awareness. We need to remember that when we look back at past events fondly, we may only remember half the story, like recalling those university days filled with friends and drinks at the student bar, and omitting how at the same time we struggled to pay the rent for an uncomfortable grotty share house. If we're not careful, the past can drag us in and make us believe that our happiest times have been and gone.

In the West, we're almost conditioned to feel sad as something ends – the end of the school holidays, the end of Christmas ('Oh, I wish it could be Christmas every day!'), watching someone we love reach their twilight years – but in doing so we miss the opportunity to celebrate what once was, and find it hard to visualise how we will cope in the aftermath. In Japanese culture, every end is a new beginning, and immersing yourself in the beauty of what is, won't make it harder to let go of something. Oftentimes, people tend to build up walls, dampening their immediate joy, protecting themselves from the eventual epilogue instead of relishing the moment. But nothing lasts forever – even the universe will come to an end someday – so appreciating each passing moment and experiencing each new encounter fully, without tenaciously grasping on to what we believe to be the most idyllic state, can help us to feel contented, even through the most turbulent times.

Cat-*sukashii*

When it comes to our feline friends, we might wonder if they can reminisce as we humans do. We have all witnessed a skittish kitty rattled by a noise that triggers a traumatic memory, but can cats recall happy memories like we do?

A small Japanese study involving forty-nine domestic cats seemed to show that felines can indeed remember pleasant experiences, such as eating a favourite treat. One of the researchers, Saho Takagi, a psychologist at Kyoto University, said cats, as well as dogs, 'used memories of a single past experience, which may imply they have episodic memory'. She explained, 'An interesting speculation is that they may enjoy actively recalling memories of their experience like humans.' Additional research shows that cats can remember for as long as ten years but are highly picky in what they select, which suggests that they only remember something that is beneficial to them. Cats remember those that care for them as well as more startling moments, such as when a vet's thermometer was shoved up their backside. Perhaps, what we can deduce from this is that it's best to recollect past moments that are advantageous to us and forget the rest.

In the book *The Courage to be Happy* by Japanese authors Ichiro Kishimi and Fumitake Koga, the two main characters debate Adlerian psychology (an approach to psychotherapy developed by Alfred Adler, a contemporary of Sigmund Freud). They discuss how 'from the innumerable events that have happened in a person's past, that person chooses only those events that are compatible with the present goals, gives meaning to them and turns them into memories'. Suggesting that we are all selective in what we remember, the characters conclude that it is not the past that dictates the now but the now that dictates the past. They raise the question, however, of why some people refer to tragedies as 'lessons' and others as 'memories', implying that while some people remain chained to past events, others don't. It's an interesting debate, and one that can aid us as we look back upon our life and question what makes our tail quiver or head hang low. Although some less positive events may be too raw for us to release immediately, if we don't handle our difficult memories with due care and attention, they can be damaging to us in our future.

Mono no aware: the ephemerality of things

Are you awestruck by the ephemeral beauty of the spring cherry blossom and the fleeting nature of things? The distinctly Japanese term for this sensation, *mono no aware*, means an 'empathy towards things' or the 'awareness of impermanence'. It highlights the importance of appreciating each moment as it is, without the need to cling to fallacious ideas of its everlasting sublimity. We touched on impermanence in Chapter F when we looked at the idea of *mujō* (impermanence or transience) in order to alleviate feelings of sadness, but in this chapter let's look at how it can make us appreciate the present before it becomes the past.

Being conscious that nothing lasts furr-ever; a bit like an expensive couch after cats have clawed it to shreds, can give you a whole new purr-spective on life. Like the *sakura* (cherry blossom) at springtime, relationships can radiantly bloom, filling our life with joy and purpose for the time they are there. Then, as seasons and people change, we begin to grieve these seemingly short-lived experiences. *Mono no aware* teaches us to remember how precious these moments were, and how privileged we are to have been a part of them. It's okay to let go of the past and allow life to continue gracefully along its natural course.

During Japan's Heian period (794–1185), the aesthetic ideal of impermanence featured prominently in the great works of art, wholly embracing the Buddhist view of the transient nature of things. It was a time of devotion to visual art, poetry and literature and most notably of *The Tale of Genji*, considered to be the world's first ever novel. Not only does the book provide a glimpse into imperial court life at this time, but it was written by a woman, Lady Murasaki, which was significant at this point in history. The novel contains examples of the fleeting nature of life and the sadness associated with it. One verse, by the character Genji, suggests how scents can resurrect old emotions of times past:

> *To this home of 'falling flower,'*
> *The odors bring thee back again,*
> *And now thou sing'st, in evening hour,*
> *Thy faithful loving strain.*

Sachiko Iwayama, author of *The Events That Shaped the History of Japan*, writes,

> In Heian-kyo the aristocrats no longer followed Chinese culture with awe, and instead began to develop their own sense of beauty. In the eighth century, people sang of plum blossoms in their poems, following the cultural taste of the Chinese people. In the ninth century, their affection shifted to the cherry blossoms – native to Japan.

I caught up with Sachiko in person to find out more about the influence this golden age of classical Japanese culture had on the country and how it helped it to mature. As we sipped green tea, Sachiko described how it was the women of the court who developed the Japanese language. She said that while student monks invented *katakana,* the women of the imperial court created *hiragana*, reducing the complicated square forms of Chinese characters into abstract rounded shapes that by the tenth century were accepted as the country's alphabet.

When I asked Sachiko about her own personal experience of *mono no aware*, she talked wistfully of visiting a mountain and being struck by the delicate cherry blossom flowers only to see them disappear a few days later like snowflakes, and the sense of life being so short and beautiful.

As the eighty-four-year-old spoke about her life and travels, which took her to Franco's Spain and Shakespeare's birthplace Stratford-upon-Avon in the mid-1960s, and they brought a smile to her face, it suddenly dawned on me that it's these seemingly unconnected moments that make up our lives. They may not appear as great works of literature, but they make up the unique narratives that define us. If we don't pay them enough care and appreciation though, they too will float away like the pink petals of the *sakura*.

Mono no aware wasn't defined as a uniquely Japanese sensibility until long after the Heian period was over, when eighteenth-century Japanese philosopher and scholar Motoori Norinaga stressed its importance through his literary criticisms of works such as *The Tale of Genji*. Since then, the concept has become deeply embedded within the culture and can be seen in manga and cinema today. One such example is the Oscar-winning Japanese film *Drive My Car*, which depicts the natural end of a relationship without the need to cling onto it, and is perhaps best described as a comment on loss and letting go. What sets it apart from Hollywood movies is that there isn't the need to end the narrative with a happy ending, because in life that is rarely the case.

Ichi-go ichi-e: treasuring each moment

While *mono no aware* is associated with the great literature of the Heian period, *ichi-go ichi-e* is said to be traced back to sixteenth-century tea master Sen no Rikyū. It means 'one chance in a lifetime'.

Ichi-go ichi-e is a Japanese idiom that describes the idea that encounters with people and opportunities are never repeated, and therefore should be treasured as a lifetime experience. You cannot hold onto one moment in time, no matter how hard you try. Even the most common everyday experiences will be slightly different each time. Think about the countless times you've sat on the couch, perhaps with a cat. Each instance comprises special elements that are unique to that particular time. Maybe the phone rang and interrupted you, or there was a knock on the door, or perhaps something less obvious, like the amount of hair the cat shed or the position it slept in. We will look more at *ichi-go ichi-e* when we consider the importance of the tea ceremony in Chapter W, but for now let's acknowledge that appreciating each moment as it happens and staying present is vital for happiness. When we do that, it's easier to look back fondly without needing to relive that moment or get lost in the memory. That way we can appreciate *natsukashii* in the same way the Japanese do. Just as a cat experiences bliss chasing after a dragonfly on a summer afternoon, a moment is fleeting and cannot be repeated, so must we be attentive when we are in the moment.

*

There are so many ways we can start practising being more present. Really take the time to feel the soft sensation of a cat's fur under your fingertips when you stroke it, or notice every delicate flavour as you sip your next cup of tea. Take a trip to the beach and pay close attention to the sensation of the salty water on your skin and the sand between your toes while you appreciate the warm breeze brushing against your face. When you see something of beauty, stare a little longer, breathe deeply, and allow yourself to slow down.

Ask yourself what *natsukashii* moments you are building today for you to look back on tomorrow and beyond with your ears pricked and a wide smile.

Oubaitōri 桜梅桃李
Never comparing oneself

No two cats in nature are exactly the same. Although they might be the same breed or from the same litter, the chances of them being completely identical in every single way is next to impossible. That's because each cat is blessed with one-off markings and individual characteristics that make them unique. Despite their fancy spotted coats, no two Egyptian maus, for example, will be indistinguishable – their gooseberry eyes might be a slightly different shade of green, or the pinkness of one's nose might not be as bright.

Yet with so many wonderful differences between us, many of us fall into the trap of comparing ourselves with others. It's hard to say whether cats develop jealousy in the same way we do, but I have witnessed my older cat size up his younger kitty counterpart as he pounces after a feathered bird toy, seemingly in awe of his athleticism.

For the Japanese, *oubaitōri* means to never compare oneself with others. The *kanji* characters that make up this word refer to four trees – the cherry, plum, peach and apricot – and the variety of growth between each one, but poetically the meaning is that every individual will bloom when they are ready.

Whether you're comparing yourself with your friends, family members, workmates or celebrities, you may not realise it at the time, but these constant comparisons can leave you feeling bereft. If you catch yourself doing this often, it might be time to consider just how much it could be affecting your sense of individualism.

The problem with comparisons

Although our feline friends might display signs of the green-eyed monster over things like food and terri-tory, they don't appear to judge themselves or others as harshly as humans do. This is because they lack the complex emotions we have. It's been said they can be good judges of character when it comes to who may cause them harm, but it's difficult to say whether they can develop their own personal inferiority complex due to some perceived notion of inadequacy, or by obses-sively comparing themselves with others.

To find out more about the concept of *oubaitōri*, I spoke with Akiko Schrader, a Japanese emotional therapist who trained under Mariko Oshino, the founder and president of the Emotional Therapy Association in Japan. We spoke about why comparing ourselves with others can cause problems. According to Akiko, the Japanese concept of *oubaitōri* suggests we shouldn't compare ourselves with others because we are all different. She explains: 'If we see people from one point of view, we judge them as "good" or as "bad", but this is not correct because everybody has both strong and weak parts that make up their character, personality and individuality. Nowadays, there is an expectation that everybody has to be good at everything, and this is flattening our individuality.' She adds: 'Every person has their own ways of seeing this world. We may all look at the same things, but every person sees it in a different way.' This is an interesting take, especially if we consider that what might be right for you might be wrong for me. No one view is correct, since it can depend on a number of variables, such as where a person comes from, their upbringing, their culture, their education, their social background, their age, their preferences, their friends and family, and even their lifestyle choices. It's worth noting here that peer pressure in Japan can be very strong and can often cause many people to suffer mentally.

There are plenty of negative effects of comparing ourselves with others, Akiko explains. 'When we compare ourselves to other people, we end up feeling sad because we normally compare our own weak points with the other person's strong points. If your life just focuses on your weak points, it means you are trying to become a different person. You should shine a light on your strong points. It's important to remember that everybody is different – and that's why we shine!'

Emotional therapy is a tool to connect to our higher self. Akiko goes on to say, 'Emotional therapy heals the negative emotions within you, and you start to love yourself, feel more confident, and remember what your soul wants to do in this life. Emotional therapy is not just about understanding your mind but feeling and experiencing, so your love of yourself and confidence will grow deeper. By using this therapy, you learn not to judge yourself or others too harshly, and begin to see situations as neutral.' After we moved on to discuss whether animals compare themselves in the same way humans do, Akiko added, 'Cats have basic emotions as well, but it's only humans that put meaning on them and try to control and decide the actions that follow.'

Jūnin toiro: ten people, ten colours

The Japanese have a saying, *jūnin toiro*, or 'ten people, ten colours', which means everyone is different and tells a different story. It poses a question: why do we bother comparing ourselves with others if we are all different to begin with? It doesn't take us long to start feeling like something is lacking when we begin to scroll through social media and see our friends or family on a luxury holiday, or spy an influencer's travel photos and feel like we want to be there too. Or when we see someone who spends all their time in the gym and begin wishing we had a body like theirs, without even considering the time and dedication it has taken them to achieve washboard abs. Flicking through photos on social media or scanning the pages of a glossy magazine won't tell you the whole story, but it's still easy to get tied up in the alluring images and feelings of want.

Since the culture we are raised in can significantly affect the way we see the world and how we experience it, does the same go for cats? In the documentary *Inside the Mind of a Cat*, experts explain interesting new research about how cats in the United States behave differently from those in Japan, and suggest that this may result from lifestyle differences between the two countries. With this in mind, it seems pointless to compare ourselves with others, since we can't fairly compare ourselves with people or situations that aren't the same, or physically change who we are or the culture we grew up in. How can you compare yourself with a Hollywood actress if you're living in a rural area somewhere outside the United States, for example? If you're always stacking yourself up against someone with a completely different lived experience, you're always setting yourself up for disappointment.

The same is true when you compare yourself with people much closer to you, such as friends or family or people who share a similar background. You might grow up on the same street as someone, or share the same parents, or go to the same school with the same teachers, but you could feel as though the outcome of your life is unfair in comparison to theirs. For many people this can develop into feelings of resentment, as if they ought to be living a similar life to their peers or siblings. But by comparing ourselves with others, we are doing ourselves a disservice. As we saw earlier, we all have our own path to follow, we will all bloom at different times, and what is right for one may not be so good for another.

Embrace your differences

Like us, cats can develop jealousy of another cat, especially if it's new and makes them feel insecure, but this tends to be associated with territory or safety rather than competing for human affection. Whether they dwell on these issues like humans do is unlikely. If you share your home with cats, you'll no doubt know how different their personalities can be.

It seems that many of us can embrace the idiosyncrasies of our cats but not of ourselves. Perfectly imperfect markings, brownish freckles on a pink nose, wayward eyes and floppy ears. Strange eating habits, odd behaviours, unusual noises. No matter the tendency or feature, these characteristic peculiarities are generally the things we celebrate in our feline friends. For us, however, not fitting in can turn into nitpicking. If you're constantly judging yourself harshly and discovering inconceivable flaws, you may need to ask why this is. Try being kinder to yourself and accepting the things you don't see as perfect, because others might love these traits in you, just as you would in your cat.

There is little value in having jealousy towards others, as it rarely offers motivation, and it will only bring you down. While some may seem like they have vast privileges compared with us, being too preoccupied with this is not beneficial. All we can do is concentrate on how we can improve our lives and those around us with the means we have. Constantly looking outwards is not the answer. Just as a plant has a process for its growth, we need first to nurture ourselves, and then wait for the right conditions if we are take root and mature. If you've ever grown anything from seed, you'll know that it takes time, patience, and the right amount of care and attention – and making sure nothing hampers it, like a cat digging up the soil around it or eating its emerging leaves. And even when all looks lost, a change of soil or fertiliser or a new position on the windowsill can make a huge difference.

In Japan, chrysanthemums represent longevity, rejuvenation and royalty, but they don't flower all year round, and neither can we. We have to accept that there will be good days as well as bad days, and this is just part of the cycle of life. When we constantly compare ourselves with others, we always come up short. If we focus on the negative parts of our lives, such as what we're missing or what we wish we had, it will only bring us down.

We should try to be aware that we rarely compare ourselves with those who have less than us, or those we believe to be in a condition worse than our own. What if we did that instead of focusing on those we think are better off? Might we become more grateful for the things we actually have? It's also worth pointing out that we don't know what anyone else is going through or experiencing, and although they might look like they have it all on their perfectly curated social media account, what is going on inside could, in reality, be dramatically different from what we imagine.

Since we're often influenced by what our friends and family think, we need to bear in mind that we're all unique, and we have our own stories. There's little benefit in getting caught up in other people's dreams if they don't suit our own. Although the urge to compare ourselves with our friends is strong, if we stay true to ourselves things will work out just fine. When we constantly compare ourselves, we fall into a trap and fail to recognise our own skills and abilities. Don't do yourself the disservice of ignoring your own talents, because in most of us these need to be coaxed and nurtured with the same care and attention we would give a seedling in order to see it bloom.

One of my favourite mantras, taught to me by yoga teacher Beth Hartig, is 'I am enough, I have enough, I do enough'. It is a simple but effective reminder that I already have all I need to be content. To be satisfied with what we have in our life and not need more is what makes us truly happy. If you constantly feel that something is lacking, then it might be time to re-evaluate things.

That's why it's sometimes a good idea to have a break from things that trigger our desires, as they can send you in the wrong direction. We need less than we think we do, and living simply away from the things we are told we should want is one way to reduce our feelings of want and need. Focus on the non-material aspects of your life for just a minute, and you'll be surprised by what you already have.

It can be tricky to focus on our own path and embrace what makes us unique, but if we take the teaching from *oubaitōri* and act more like plants that grow at their own speed rather than racing to be like others, we may start to slow down and blossom at a much more manageable pace. When we're in full bloom it becomes infectious, and just as a beautiful bouquet of flowers can brighten up a room, being content with who you are will impact those around you, and if you have one, your cat too.

Pari shōkōgun パリ症候群
Dealing with disappointment

Imagine you've waited months counting down the days for your well-deserved holiday, booked your cat into a luxurious cattery, and spent hours poring over the internet to find the perfect *ryokan* (inn) in a quaint Japanese city, only to find on arrival that you have to sleep on the floor and share the bathroom. Do you immediately let it ruin your holiday and give in to your feelings of disappointment by creating a story about 'what if'– or do you look for happiness in the beautiful old inn with great service and a hot spring?

Paris syndrome

To illustrate our next teaching, in this chapter we'll be looking at a term coined by Japanese psychiatrist Hiroaki Ota, which describes a severe form of culture shock. The term *Pari shōkōgun,* or Paris syndrome, can be traced back to Ota's work at the Sainte-Anne Hospital Center in France in the 1980s. Ota had witnessed that many Japanese tourists who visited the French capital with great hopes of fancy patisseries and high-end designer clothes would often become hugely disappointed, many of them experiencing psychiatric symptoms such as delusions, hallucinations and anxiety. So great is the disappointment of *Pari shōkōgun* that the Japanese Embassy is reportedly on hand to assist visitors experiencing serious episodes.

One person who experienced Paris syndrome in this way is Japanese graphic designer Shigeo Kondo-Maher, who travelled all the way from Kyoto to the UK via Paris with his partner and their dog, Gilly. Of his arrival in the City of Light, he said, 'When I landed in Paris, I was so overwhelmed. It wasn't the Paris of my dreams.' Behind these intense feelings of disappointment is perhaps the romanticisation of France, which in the Japanese language is the only country to receive the honorific *o-* prefix – when they say *o-furansu* – which is usually reserved for native Japanese words to show respect, such as *o-kome* (お米, rice), *o-kane* (お金, money), or *o-sake* (お酒, sake). Shigeo's explanation for this is that 'Japanese people think of France as the poshest, most sophisticated country in the world, and use it as a sort of *keigo*'.

Keigo is one of the ways the Japanese show politeness, respect or humility through their speech. It can cause confusion for those learning the language, but is a necessary element of the culture. It exists to show consideration for elders or those in of higher social standing, and is again a good example of how Japanese culture focuses on social harmony, as we saw in Chapter C and examine in more detail in the next chapter.

When I asked Shigeo how his pet helped ease the difficulties of settling in to a new country, he explained: 'Moving into a new community with Gilly is such a great way to be a part of a local neighbourhood. Especially if you are in the countryside, you'll always find a new doggy friend. The only problem is that you'll have to memorise all the dog's names, and you'll often forget to ask the dog owner's name!'

Although pets can be a great aid in helping us adjust to a new place, not everyone has a cat or dog for comfort, and it isn't always possible to bring our furry friends along on every adventure. So how else can we cope when we find it hard to settle in to a new place because we're faced with difficult feelings about the unknown?

I spoke with Sam Fujii, the managing director of a duty-free shop for Japanese tourists located close to the world-famous Great Barrier Reef in Australia. Sam gets to see many tourists pass through his Fujii Store, so

I asked him his opinion on travellers' expectations and how best to deal with feelings of unease in a new place or situation. He said, 'Firstly, ten people are ten colours, so not everybody likes the same things. We are all different, and that's okay. Most Japanese tourists expect to meet koalas and kangaroos when they come to Australia, and may get disappointed if they don't. I think as far as Cairns is concerned, it's a World Heritage Site, so they have high hopes for it.'

Sam goes on to say what tourists should do when their expectations of a place are sometimes different from reality: 'People have different ways of thinking, so there may not be one correct way to do things. I think the important thing is to understand each other and interact with each other as much as possible.'

While Paris syndrome is usually connected to the Japanese in France, it can happen to foreigners visiting Japan as well. One example is British writer Angela Carter, who wrote in her book *Fireworks* of her initial experience in Japan: 'The city, the largest in the world, the city designed to suit not one of my European expectations.' Similar to Carter's, my arrival in Osaka did not create the euphoria I'd been expecting. Instead, my first impressions were of grey treeless streets, language barriers and constant food challenges. You could describe the look on my face when I arrived, as the Japanese say, as 'like the face of a cat blowing tea' (as if to cool it). It's not that I didn't like the city or the people, more that it wasn't living up to my expectations of cherry blossoms and cat cafes. Landing on a man-made island in Japan's steel-grey Osaka Bay, which is rimmed by vast concrete neighbourhoods, was a far cry from the snow-capped mountains and towering cedar trees in an ancient forest I had envisaged. Did I allow it to ruin my plans? Unfortunately, yes, I did. But the lessons I learned from these unmet expectations were more valuable than you might think.

For example, transitioning over to Japanese cuisine was complicated. The most common answer to my requests for non-meat dishes was, 'This one is vegetarian but with bacon.' It took me a while to discover restaurants that had picture menus so I could point and order, and usually a dish would arrive that almost resembled what I'd ordered. This was a valuable lesson in not only acceptance, but also understanding that my options didn't have to be limited to either a yes or a no, which in the past would have resulted in either a massive high or a serious low for me. Now I began to see an array of possibilities presenting themselves, and although in the end I might not always get what I wanted, I did get what I needed at the time.

My initial feeling of apprehension towards life in the city left me to experience my own version of culture shock, which I named 'Osaka syndrome', but had I not stuck it out in Japan, I would have missed out on adopting a stray cat that changed my life, countless opportunities to meet amazing people who have become lifelong friends, discovering my *ikigai*, and learning so many lessons from a culture quite different from my own.

Often, our fixed views can hamper our experiences, and result in us being less open to unexpected opportunities. So the next time you're in a fancy restaurant and you're told your favourite main is unavailable, see it as an opportunity to try something new.

When faced with these types of disappointments, we need to be more cat-like in our approach and adapt to our surroundings with less fuss and more resolve, letting go of our preconceived expectations. Our fixed ideas about how things should be and our need for perfection may dampen our experience, but if we allow ourselves to veer slightly off course, we create room to explore more things. Like, for me, the discovery of *shōjin ryōri*, otherwise known as Buddhist cuisine, a plant-based meal eaten by monks that for the most part solved my dietary issues when I chose to dine out.

This mindset is not only limited to food though. It could mean putting your ideas about foreign cinema aside so that you can agree on what movie to watch with your partner, or trying to remain calm when your favourite beauty product is discontinued. Opening yourself up to change will allow you to experience new things – and who knows, you might like your new discovery more. Although it might feel like the world has ended when a shop no longer stocks your favourite brand, or the hotel room you've booked in France doesn't have views of the

Eiffel Tower, you might just discover an unknown treat, like a gorgeous Parisian cafe hiding on the doorstep of your back-alley hotel, filled with friendly locals.

Giving yourself room to explore new things can also enable you to become more mindful of your reactions. It's interesting to monitor them and notice how you feel when you wanted A but got B. How do you cope when your expectations aren't met? Does it leave you feeling triggered? Our approach to these frustrations makes all the difference.

Dealing with disappointment

Like us, cats are likely to experience disappointment in certain situations, such as when their bowl is empty, feeding times are changed or they can't go outside. Even though they can't speak, cats are good at getting across how disappointed they feel about things. Whether it's the unopened gap in the window, an empty bowl at meal-times, or an insufficient amount of attention, they'll make their displeasure known by stepping on their owner's keyboard, meowing noisily by the door, or clawing at the carpet.

The difference between us and our feline overlords is that they are less likely to let these things ruin their day, eventually returning to their basket for a quick cat nap and waking up in a different mood altogether. Felines are masters of letting things go. They don't doubt their decisions, waste time second-guessing, or ruin their present by lingering over what-ifs; rather, they keep things in purr-spective and carry on, fairly positive that the next time they head for a cuddle they'll comfortably curl up in their owner's lap, and that if they make a dash for freedom the cat flap will open and their wish will be granted.

*

Although disappointing experiences might seem disagreeable at the time, they can make you stronger if you allow them to. You'll not only become more equipped with dealing with the unknown, but you'll know how you can handle these types of situations in the future. Cats accept reality as it is, and don't constantly try to control things. The stress and anxiety that come with disappointment are as strong as you allow them to be, and although it may not seem like it at the time, if we take a leaf out of a cat's book and don't let our expectations get the better of us, we'll be better for it. You never know, there could even be a teaching in the disappointment you experience.

In the words of the Dalai Lama, 'If you have too much expectation, you may come away disappointed.'

R

Reigi 礼儀
Etiquette and manners

Have you met the kind of cat that vomits chunks of grass all over the Persian rug rather than doing it neatly on the ground outside? Perhaps they need a lesson in etiquette and good manners. *Reigi* affects all aspects of Japanese life, and it teaches us about respect and living more harmoniously. Used, for example, in judo, it is a way to seek self-improvement and contribute to society.

As we have explored in earlier chapters, etiquette is deeply embedded in Japanese culture. Almost every action has a certain set of rules or proper procedure, and failure to comply with this norm has the potential to be seen as disrespectful and disruptive.

Reigi translates as politeness, courtesy, manners and etiquette, and is used to describe how things ought to be done in order to show good conduct and behaviour – such as using formal greetings or correct speech, dressing appropriately, honouring others, and not disagreeing with someone you don't know well, or interrupting someone when they're talking, especially your boss. It's interesting to note that according to research, politeness may not necessarily mean the same thing to everyone, and in Japan, as we will see, greater importance appears to be placed on showing respect, hierarchy and modesty.

While *jōshiki* (see Chapter J) is primarily concerned with knowledge that is common, *reigi* is a way of thinking, speaking and acting that respects others in order to avoid trouble. For example, the act of bowing, or *ojigi*, is a well-known way to show courtesy and respect in Japan, albeit one that can cause outsiders to feel confused. In a country with such a strict hierarchical structure, it is essential to be well mannered to ensure acceptance within the confines of the culture. Failure to do so could leave you red-faced. Even the different degrees of bowing could potentially cause embarrassment, such as doing a nod bow to someone of high ranking instead of the *saikeirei*, which is a deeply reverent forty-five- to seventy-degree bow. It all depends on the situation, which takes outsiders time to get to grips with, but as a central part of the culture, these customs are necessary to learn.

At first glance, the nightly newsreaders bowing on NHK (the Japan Broadcasting Corporation), might seem overly formal and rigid, yet given how less fractured this culture appears to be than some others, it might be worth considering how these customs work to provide not just conformity, but cooperation. Similar to the cooperation I witnessed between the courteous cats at a nature park in Tochigi, which show a kind awareness of each other. Instead of acting on their every single desire, these Japanese cats recognise their fellow felines and avoid tensions by respecting each other's space.

Cats can be seen demonstrating polite behaviour elsewhere in Japan. The NHK documentary *A Cat's-Eye View of Japan*, by wildlife photographer and filmmaker Mitsuaki Iwagō, follows Maro, a kitty that lives at a pottery store in Aichi, which is a town famous for making cat figurines. He follows the cat's daily life spent resting in the sun, grooming himself, and politely responding to the pats of customers. Strangely, unlike some other cats, Maro suppresses his instincts to knock any of the pottery items on the floor or behave in a manner that might disrupt the day-to-day running of the business, despite any innate temptation for cat-like mischief.

Being polite can promote harmonious relationships, since you are not only showing respect, but also avoiding conflict through maintaining boundaries, and choosing your words carefully. For example, using honorific speech ensures no one is offended. We previously looked at how *annei* (Chapter A), *enryo* (Chapter E) and *jōshiki* (Chapter J) can help towards achieving a peaceful society, how having a reserved attitude can prevent conflict through self-control, and how the common sense of people and subtle nuances in conduct can be beneficial to the smooth running of things. Now let's consider *reigi* and cats in more depth.

I'm Tsushima the Cat

Cats are reserved creatures; rarely do they bother others or deliberately cause offence. They seem mindful of their surroundings, and are receptive if their humans act politely towards them. They seem particularly gifted at training their owners to be thoughtful and attentive to their needs, without being rude or displaying overly demanding behaviour – unless you neglect to feed them on time, which may result in a gentle ankle bite as a reminder you have slacked off.

In the first episode of the Japanese manga series *Ore, Tsushima* (*I'm Tsushima the Cat*) by Opūnokyōdai, our feline lead perfectly displays *reigi* in action. When Tsushima is introduced to his new feline foster family for the first time, he uses a very formal greeting, leaving the other cats impressed by his bow and politeness. They say to Tsushima *Reigi tadashii* when they meet him, showing how much they appreciate his demonstration of correct and proper *reigi*. Surprisingly though, this well-mannered cat, who even says that he will sit in the corner so as not to upset the other house felines, has quite a different attitude when it comes to his new human carer, crazy cat person Ojii-chan.

This series expresses the appeal of cats in a deep and accurate way but with comic levity. At first Tsushima, whose past life as a street cat has led him to develop a wariness of humans, appears to be rude to his human rescuer, pretending to sleep when called upon to fight off an attacking bee, and threatening to leave when things don't go his way, knowing that it would break Ojii-chan's heart if he did. It takes considerable time for this former stray to trust the person who kindly rescued him, but even with mistrust, Tsushima remains respectful. In spite of his brash demeanour, Tsushima acts with courtesy around the house, acknowledging the longest-serving foster cat, Zun, as the most important in the house, and avoiding meaningless fights with any other cats when conflict arises. As the series progresses and Tsushima's time at Ojii-chan's house goes on, Tsushima even shows gentle affection for the human character. This is beautifully illustrated in an episode where an unfamiliar stray enters the home and Tsushima declares that he will protect his carer as if it was his duty.

Another demonstration of the importance of honour and respect occurs in an episode involving a heated exchange between Ojii-chan and the pet sitter. Ojii-chan accuses the pet sitter of not showing Tsushima the Cat enough respect when she omits the polite Japanese suffix *san*. In the previous chapter, we saw how the *o-* prefix can be used to show respect for a word. The humorous discussion that ensues about the correct title of respect for a cat illustrates the importance of using honorifics in Japan, and shows how if used appropriately, they can help to build good relationships in daily life.

Jun Tagami from Inner Nature, whom we met in Chapter M when exploring *mottainai*, says of the manga series, 'I thought that this is a clumsy expression of love.' He explains, 'One of the most important ideas in Bushidō, or way of the samurai warrior, is *rei*, and what they are saying here is that politeness is meaningless if it is just a formality.' In that sense, politeness needs to be earned, but while this animation ignores formality, at its heart is sincerity. Jun adds, 'Sincerity is also one of the seven virtues of Bushidō. In that sense, this cat is like a samurai. As Confucius once said, "Without sincerity and honesty, courtesy is a farce".'

Cats and hierarchy

You are not alone in chuckling at the well-known saying 'Dogs have owners, cats have staff', which might conjure up images of feline grandeur, but perhaps in reality cats are only asking for what all of us want, which is the respect and attention we all deserve. While it's unclear if cats follow rules and etiquette in the same way we do, they know how to politely co-exist together, purposely giving space to other members of a group and exhibiting good social graces – until a new cat shows up. While many cat behaviour experts agree that there is no social hierarchy among cats, others say there is still a pecking order. I spoke with American author and cat behaviourist Allison Hunter-Frederick to find out more.

She says, 'Scent communication is vital for cats to interact without conflict because cats become comfortable with each other by creating a group scent. They create a group scent by marking, which is done in a variety of ways. Indoor cats will scent mark by using litter boxes and scratching posts and by rubbing against objects, people, and each other with their scent glands.'

Many feline behaviour experts now believe that the social structure of cats is not a linear hierarchy. Instead, they are thought to have complex relationships and interact using social graces. Allison adds, 'Many cat experts believe that there is no such thing as a cat hierarchy but instead cats can form social groups. Based on the observations of feral cat colonies, cat experts believe that while feral cats are solitary hunters, small groups of females and kittens can form colonies based around available food sources. These colonies will then establish individual hunting territories, which they scent mark in order to minimise conflict within their groups.'

It's been well documented that cats use body language, vocalisation, and marking to form loose 'agreements' with each other over who inhabits which part of a home at certain times of the day, and will also politely take it in turn to use different resources indicating an awareness of one another in the same way Tsushima the cat did in the anime series.

So, are cats polite? Allison says yes and no. Cats have mannerisms that could be viewed as both polite and impolite. She says, 'Cats will slow-blink to show acceptance or friendliness. Another possible sign of politeness is that cats will take turns using essential resources and favourite resting spaces.'

In the same way that people have mannerisms that could be viewed as impolite, cats also do too. Allison concludes by saying, 'They might stare down an opponent to show dominance or use signs of aggression over disputed territory. And while most cats often avoid tension by respecting each other's spaces, this isn't always the case.'

Shitashiki naka ni mo reigi ari: politeness towards all

The Japanese proverb *Shitashiki naka ni mo reigi ari*, which translates as 'Even intimates should be polite with each other' might cause at least a bit of an eye-roll among some of the younger generation, but this phrase could perhaps hold some valuable lessons if examined more deeply.

When we let our guard down with people and make the leap from being acquaintances to becoming friends, or closer, many of us find it difficult to set boundaries. This often results in people crossing the line, such as one person taking advantage of another's good will, which could lead to resentment within the relationship. Sometimes this is done innocently enough, and not necessarily out of spite, but instead due to a misunderstanding of the other person's limitations thanks to poor communication. When we don't remain mindful of not giving or taking too much, it could affect our own or another's health. While we don't need to mark our territory in the way cats do, the beauty of boundaries is that they can help prevent any unwanted aggression further down the track. Neither cats nor people enjoy the hissing and yowling that comes with invaded territory or feeling overburdened or threatened, so the best thing to do is avoid conflict before it begins.

Gentle boundary setting can help prevent unnecessary tension, and this is where *reigi* can help. When you're clear about what you want and what you don't want and can use polite speech to get your point across, it's likely that you won't ruffle anyone's fur. While codes of conduct seem rigid and sometimes unnecessary, they can help create a universal language through which we can aim for improvement of both ourselves and our relationships with others, without feeling threatened or unsure. Ultimately, used correctly, proper etiquette can allow us to develop discipline and respect where we might otherwise be controlled by our emotions, which in turn leads to fewer complications in life.

Being polite and well mannered can separate us from those who operate only to cause offence, and can create a calm and welcoming environment for those who are struggling to find emotional stability within themselves. It might not come as second nature to everyone, but with practice and patience – for ourselves and with others – we can develop new habits that could allow us to form deeper connections with those around us. Through discipline and respect, *reigi* can teach us self-improvement, structure and compassion. Bringing our awareness to our actions can help us to understand that our choices could have an impact on how another person (or cat) feels. We want to avoid acting selfishly, but as Jun pointed out, being polite without sincerity is pointless and could ultimately lead to resentment. Instead, we should aim to interact with others with the type of courtesy we wish to be shown.

Holding a door open for someone instead of letting it swing back into their face, thanking the bus driver before you leave, or queuing patiently without hurrying the person in front of you, are versions of etiquette-based peacekeeping in English-speaking nations. Some could view these conventions as stuffy or outdated, but when we choose to adhere to them it's because we care about how the other person feels, and we'd hope to be granted the same courtesy should the tables be turned.

*

Japanese bowing protocols and honorific speech can help to generate a mutual kindness between people. It's about more than just a set of rules and structure or making sure you get off on the right foot. *Reigi* is a sincere expression of respect that comes from the heart, and is fundamental to operating with intention, showing restraint over knee-jerk reactions, and reducing complications and confusion within relationships. In the same way, cats that live in a shared space use social graces to prevent conflict, and by incorporating *reigi* into your life you can ease tension and create a more harmonious way of living.

Seijaku & Shizen 静寂 自然
Stillness & Naturalness

If a cat were demonstrating signs of obsession or compulsion towards a particular activity, you'd probably think something was amiss, like a behavioural disorder or some kind of illness. For humans, though, it seems perfectly socially acceptable for us to mindlessly engage in repetitive activities without any specific purpose other than to avoid being still.

Think of the number of times you pick up your smartphone to scroll through social media, get lost watching a string of videos on YouTube, or manically clean your house to avoid something. You get the picture. Perhaps we humans could do with wearing an Elizabethan collar around our necks like cats do after a visit to the vet. But instead of stopping us from licking our wounds, it would prevent us from overusing gadgets or intentionally busy-bodying, helping us to enjoy more moments of peace and tranquillity.

The Japanese have a deep appreciation for the value of simplistic silence and reconnecting with nature, and so do cats. When a kitty lies across your chest, rendering you immovable, they could be trying to send you a message that perhaps you need more moments of stillness in your life. If the only stillness you experience is when a cat lies on top of you so that you can't budge, maybe it's time for you to do things a little differently and try to resist the urge to always be busy and distracted.

Seijaku, which means 'the silence found in nature (or our mind)', is another of the Seven Japanese Aesthetic Principles (*wabi-sabi*) we will consider in this book. As the famous quote from thirteenth-century Persian poet and philosopher Rumi goes, 'The quieter you become, the more you are able to hear.'

Seeking *seijaku*

Inside a centuries-old temple, far away from distractions, I was able to find the stillness I had been lacking for so long. It can be hard to achieve a quiet mind in today's technologically connected world, where we are constantly chasing our tails over algorithm updates and verification codes, and fighting the urge to doom-scroll – even though we know we never feel good about it afterwards. It can be difficult to remind ourselves of the importance of finding some time for ourselves, and seeking silence away from digital disturbances and our seemingly never-ending quest to get things done. It wasn't until I had the experience of meditating in an ancient shrine room with the faint lingering smell of incense that had been burnt for centuries that I understood just how still I could be. Being away from familiar surroundings and liberated from the usual daily grind meant that this mountain meditation came far more easily for me than when I was at home.

To sit quietly might sound easy, but it can be a difficult task for most of us. Sitting still and being alone with ourselves can often cause our minds to do the exact opposite of keeping quiet. That's because many of us spend the vast majority of our lives living up in our heads, and reconnecting with our body is largely foreign. Instead of allowing ourselves to feel what we feel, we end up thinking and analysing. Yet being able to think without attaching meaning or judgement is a virtue of meditative practices – it's the art of allowing our thoughts to just be, without giving them any attention or intention. It's a hard task, especially for those people who have spent their whole lives distracting themselves from thoughts that are too painful to face. Distractions can then become comforting habits, like overeating, overworking, overuse of digital devices, and any addictive behaviour a person might use to avoid stillness. But stillness can allow our thoughts to flow more freely by releasing an overburdened mind.

For me, it has taken years of erratic practice and it rarely comes easily. With patience, though, sitting still and reflecting is when we can be most at peace with ourselves.

I asked Tomoko Gregory, a yoga teacher with many years of experience, about how we can find stillness in everyday life. She says, 'Wherever we live, if our mind is busy or stressful, we can't find the stillness and tranquillity we need. Through yoga, including breathing practice, we will master how we restrict our consciousness. Imagine there is a lake inside our bodies. If we react to something that happens around us, the water of the lake becomes like the waves of an ocean. If we don't react and just wait, the water of the lake stays calm.'

Finding peace within ourselves through moments of stillness could regenerate our resilience so that we can continue to take on the things that happen around us without losing ourselves in the process. When I asked Tomoko-san what she thinks we can learn from our animals about stillness, she explained, 'They are in this moment without thinking like we do. They don't lie to themselves. Their mind and action are the same.' She then went on to share a story about her guinea pig, Ham. 'He was my mentor. I believe that all life has a spirit.

After he passed away, I felt his spirit more than before, as I couldn't see his body. He was on my chest for about two hours very peacefully then passed away. When he died suddenly, he stretched his body and became stiff. I felt like the electricity was moving through his body and his spirit flew up to the sky. He taught me how we should live and die.'

Tomoko-san added, 'When we worry about the future or think back to the past, we have stress. Mainly, we are not able to be happy because we are not in the moment. When we are with animals we don't talk about the future or the past. We can be in this moment with mindfulness by spending time with animals.'

The importance of non-doing

We touched on the importance of non-doing in Chapter C when demonstrating the importance of finding balance with yin and yang, and since ancient times religious leaders, as well as cats, have espoused the importance of stillness. The need to pause and reflect is often forgotten in today's hectic world, but it's even more essential in this day and age.

Cats are masters of non-doing, and rarely do they interfere in another cat's business. Perhaps there's something to be learned from this feline approach to inaction. Pouring yourself a green tea and sitting down to enjoy it is an easy way to find stillness in daily life. So too is lazing on your back and staring at the sky. We don't need to be on holiday or somewhere outstanding to allow ourselves these small pleasures. We can do something as simple as sit somewhere quiet and dangle our feet in cool clear water to quieten our mind.

Beyond the daily benefits of taking some time out for ourselves, sitting quietly and reflecting, the Chinese Taoist concept of *wu-wei*, or effortless action (attributed to Lao-Tzu, the reputed author of the *Tao Teh Ching*, and founder of philosophical Taoism), suggests that there should be no interference or no wilful action in what we do.

This concept might seem alien to some, since we're constantly striving for more and more in our lives. But what if we were to allow things to unfold naturally and release our desire to control every aspect of our waking lives? Most would say that we'd never achieve anything if that were the case, and often I'd be inclined to agree with them. Yet, as Jason Gregory points out in his book *Effortless Living*, 'Many people seek to control life down to the finest detail, failing to realize that the very things that shaped their identity were beyond their control.'

What if we were to loosen our grip a little? Would everything turn out okay? If you find your tendency to meddle in things doesn't generally result in the desired outcome, then perhaps it's time to let go of some of your original concepts. It's worth pondering whether incessantly controlling every aspect of your waking life is really necessary, and whether over-managing everything could be causing us more harm than good.

Let's consider how much control cats have over their day. They don't keep digital diaries or plan appointments weeks in advance, they just let things unfold. Of course, plans can be useful, but there are so many external factors influencing our lives that we can't control, and obsessively trying to plan every aspect of something can pull us away from our true intentions. It can also prevent us from seeing the potential beauty in things and allowing the mystery of life to unfold naturally. Think about the number of times you check your inbox for a response that may never be coming, instead of spending quality time with your loved ones. Or a time you might have missed a night out with friends to work on a project you'd been hammering for days and could probably use a break from anyway.

Sometimes inaction can have its benefits and give us the clarity of mind we've been missing when we're overwhelmed with perpetual doing. My best creative ideas usually come when I'm somewhere quiet, away from my usual life, like on a walk or on holiday. I generally have one of those a-ha moments when I'm far away from my laptop and everything miraculously pieces together seamlessly. But when there's too much going on and I'm huddled over my computer mindlessly doing, juggling, multitasking and switching between a million ideas in my overly cluttered mind, things don't seem so clear and the creative well runs dry.

Shizen: naturalness

Next, we'll look at *shizen* – also pronounced *jinen* – which, like *seijaku*, falls under the Seven Aesthetic Principles of *wabi-sabi*. Embracing this ancient philosophy can offer you not only a shift in perspective, but also add more meaning to your day-to-day life.

With a focus on being in harmony with nature rather than seeing it as something to conquer or change, *shizen* teaches us about acceptance and interconnection. Although it might sound like a cliché, where better to find beauty and stillness than in a forest tucked away from the pulsating sounds of *pachinko* (gaming) parlours, their noisy slot machines or the incessant hum of city traffic?

Living close to places like Kamikōchi, deep in the heart of the Japanese Alps, a sacred highland with clear rivers and untouched beauty, I felt more at ease, as if I was becoming more and more intertwined with nature rather than separate from it. *Shinrin-yoku* or forest bathing is practised widely in Japan, and is highly regarded due to its therapeutic benefits. It's something I enjoyed regularly in Japan – even with a cat in tow. Walking through the picturesque landscape filled with Japanese cedars, red pines and cypress trees helped me to unwind, and by paying attention to what surrounded me in the moment, such as the unique sound made by the Japanese green woodpecker and its incomparable beauty, I experienced a quiet calm that I never could in a busy city. To recognise the beauty in nature for what it is, without the need to interfere, is not something many of us are used to. Unfortunately, nature is often seen as something to capitalise on and destroy in the process.

When I asked Tomoko-san what we can learn from the concept of *shizen*, she said, 'Everything is circulating in nature. Human beings are not in the circle in modern society. We have to think how we can put ourselves back into the circle. For example, one day I was watching the grapefruit tree in the garden. That tree is growing without leaning on the other trees of the garden. It becomes tall and strong then grows leaves, flowers and fruits. The tree is happy to share the fruits with other animals. Some of its fruits fall down to the ground and make the soil under the tree rich. The surrounding trees are growing well because of the richness of the soil. We have to remember that the sun is shining and gives us life, and that nature is all-giving.'

If we escape the artificiality of life by embracing the naturalness of things, we will be better able to coexist with nature rather than destroy it. In the process, we will become more accepting of ourselves and others through realising that we're not separate from each other but connected, and we will be still like the trees in the forest.

Shibumi: understated beauty

Let's end this chapter with a brief look at *shibumi*. This word is often used to describe refined quality and beauty that is not flashy but subtle, deep and elegant for a wide variety of things, from art, design and fashion to situations, people and objects. It can even be positive or negative, depending on the context. *Shibumi* is the noun, while *shibui* is the adjective used to describe things, people or places.

Although it is hard to pin this concept down with one English word (one of its varied meanings describes the characteristic nature of the juice of a persimmon), the interpretation that perhaps fits best with our focus here is a quality of 'calm insightfulness' or 'effortless perfection'. For cats, perhaps imagine a beautiful stray feline that has a gnarly scar on its face – this could be considered *shibui*.

When applied to people, the idea of *shibui* could range from modesty to naturalness, everydayness and an elegant simplicity – perhaps someone like George Clooney might come to mind. Japanese people often say '*shibui otoko*' to describe a stylish older man. The Japanese actor Hideaki Itō could be another good illustration of the word.

In his book *Shibumi*, Trevanian describes the concept as 'spiritual tranquillity that is not passive; it is being without the angst of becoming'. This notion of relinquishing the need to control or overanalyse will result in greater stillness or 'overwhelming calm', as it has been described. In other words, it is a 'less is more' type of approach. Of course, the real test is being able to take the stillness you gain from being in a forest or meditating with you wherever you go, and not overcomplicating things with too many thoughts or a desire to control, but instead enjoying the silent stillness. When we're so caught up in our lives, constantly distracted and excessively consuming, we miss what's truly important and ignore the charm found in subtleties.

While most of us don't live in a landscape of fluffy white clouds – unlike Sanjūrō, the resident 'cat lord' at Bitchū Matsuyama Castle, one of the highest-altitude castles in Japan – we can still find the conditions to practise stillness in our everyday lives, if we allow ourselves.

*

Japanese Zen aesthetics offer us a different way of thinking about the world, and can guide us to a more graceful way of living. If we try to watch things unfold rather than constantly micromanaging every single detail, we may feel less discomfort when the things we want don't materialise. That's not to say that we shouldn't aim for things in life, of course – we should have goals and dreams that we can work towards – but perhaps surrendering a little more to the things we can't control and opening ourselves up to the possibility that things will unfold as they will regardless of how much we struggle and stress, could leave us feeling a greater sense of calm. We'll look more of the idea of surrendering control in Chapter U on *unmei* (destiny).

But for now, let's finish with the words of the seventeenth-century Japanese haiku master Bashō Matsuo: 'Sitting quietly, doing nothing, spring comes, and the grass grows, by itself.'

T

Torimodosu 取り戻す
Bouncing back

Some cats will willingly flop over to expose their soft bellies for a blissful tickle, no matter the tickler, and others would sooner scratch at the hand that feeds them. Often the latter kitties have been subjected to something painful in their past and are reluctant to trust again. Humans react very similarly, creating narratives through experience, some of which hold us back. For those of us who have been hurt badly before, it can be a long journey trying to regain the type of confidence needed to bounce back and feel safe in the knowledge that more bad things aren't waiting just around the corner.

Similar to the English saying 'When life knocks you down, dust yourself off and get back up again', the verb *torimodosu* can mean to find strength after something unexpected happens, such as losing a loved one or separating from a partner.

Even in our darkest moments, if we are able to rise up, put one paw in front of the other, and keep on walking, we may be able to reclaim the peace we once had. While coping with the deep feelings of sadness that come with these traumatic events may seem like an impossibility, it's worth remembering that just as gloomy days will eventually pass, if we keep trying, brighter days will surely come.

In this chapter, we'll take a deeper look at how the language we use can impact the specific narratives we create for ourselves, and more specifically the power of words when we focus on *kotodama* – the Japanese belief that words have spirits – but first let's consider cats and *torimodosu*.

Tabbies and *torimodosu*

It's difficult to know whether cats feel sadness over abandonment or the loss of a home, or if they mourn the death of a feline friend or their owner's passing in the same way we do – but there have been countless stories of cats displaying their grief in various ways. I witnessed firsthand my tabby Lulu's altered behaviour when her boyfriend, Shinsei, passed away. Lulu's sadness manifested as late-night restlessness, a significant loss of appetite (for a puss who loved her food), and a huge drop-off in her inclination to play or interact. Despite these changes in her behaviour, it would still be impossible for me to truly understand what my cat was feeling during her period of what I would call bereavement, but what remains clear is that cats seemingly have the ability to return to normal life faster than we do. I spoke with Takako Saito, the owner of Asakusa Nekoen, or Rescue Cat Cafe, in Tokyo, about how our feline friends are so efficient at finding strength after something unexpected happens.

Whenever I am in Japan, I try to visit this place because of the wonderful work Takako-san does. While some cat cafes are for entertainment purposes only, this one not only rescues and rehomes, but also educates visitors about cat welfare. Since opening in 2009, Takako has had 300–400 cats successfully adopted, and because she has seen so many felines who've experienced traumatic events – particularly those who lost their owners and their homes in the tragic events of the 2011 Tōhoku earthquake and tsunami – she's observed how kitties cope better than most. She says, 'Even though cats sustain terrible emotional trauma from being abandoned by their past owners, if the new owner is patient and treats them kindly, they can learn to trust humans again. Cats are creatures who know a very pure kind of love.'

We spoke about the cats of Fukushima, and how compared with normal city street cats, they were able to adjust to a new indoor life at a slightly quicker pace. Takako said, 'The Fukushima cats have not experienced mistreatment at human hands, so they are relatively tamer and quicker to become incredibly friendly. City cats are taught by their mamas to stay away from humans, so it can take months for them to overcome their wariness, especially if they are captured as adults.'

I asked how cats are able to bounce back after they have been abandoned or have lost their owners. She said, 'Cats are extremely careful and cautious creatures. When a cat has never experienced life with humans before, at first they will usually lash out and try to punch you.

'But if you keep at it, caring for them and talking with them every day, eventually their hearts will open to you. It may sometimes take years. I believe that living with humans is embedded in cats' genetic code, so they will inevitably become accepting and friendly.'

Speaking of her motivation to rescue and rehome kitties in need, Takako said, 'All cats in Japan originally come from house cats. We call them "stray cats" because someone threw them away, and the authorities euthanase them when they multiply too much in the wild.

'But that is not their fault. There is no such thing as a life that is created only to be killed, and no life should be destroyed by humans at a whim. We humans must take responsibility, as cats cannot live without humans.'

When I asked if cats are especially resilient and what we can learn from them, she went on to say, 'Cats are tough. Even after being discarded by humans, they fight desperately to stay alive outdoors through the heat, cold, fear, hunger, thirst and loneliness. Even so, in Japan the average life expectancy of a street cat is estimated to be just two to three years. By comparison, the average for indoor domestic cats is sixteen years. No matter how hard they fight, cats cannot survive outdoors in this world without human help.'

Like a city cat teaching her kittens the dangers of humans, we too learn to be cautious through traumatic events. This learned wariness keeps vulnerable cats alive, but our human tendency to make mountains out of molehills can have a powerful impact on our behaviour. When we struggle to bounce back, or overcompensate by putting up walls, we could potentially be sacrificing our overall wellbeing. As Takako says, a mistreated stray will struggle to survive in the world alone without the help of a kind human. If we can learn from the cats of Asakusa Nekoen and open our hearts to the love and help of our family and friends, we too can find the strength to bounce back.

Kotodama: words have spirits

Since how we think can affect how we feel, it's important to stay curious about the way we respond to certain difficulties, especially if we have a tendency to assign strong negative labels to things, people or situations. Not only can this impact our emotions, but there is evidence to suggest that it can also affect our physiological response in a way that perpetuates these powerful negative emotions.

Kotodama is a Japanese term meaning 'word-spirit'. It is the spiritual belief in the 'power of words' – the idea that if you say certain things, you may attract certain things. The ancient Japanese believed that mystical powers dwell in words and can have a dramatic impact on us, bringing about what was uttered, which teaches us that we should be mindful of their use.

I asked Nana Tomihara, a linguist and language support officer with the North Queensland Regional Aboriginal Corporation Languages Centre, more about this fascinating concept. She said, '*Kotodama* is a belief that uttering a thought breathes life into it.' Many of us are familiar with the concept of the power of words, integrating practices like affirmations or mantras in our daily routines to attract positivity. According to Nana, 'If you say positive words, you can attract positive things and if you say negative things, you attract negative things in life. It is still a very popular thought today in Japan, at least around me. My mother used to tell me not to say, "I am poor".'

Nana went on to say, 'Of course this is a spiritual belief, but I personally think it is to do with human psychology as well. If you do research on the power of words in psycholinguistic papers, you probably will find the science behind it.'

When I asked Nana why she believes words can have such a powerful effect on people, she replied, 'Words and thoughts/beliefs are closely related. Words represent how people think and believe, since languages are communication tools. Of course, words not only represent people's thoughts and beliefs but also shape people's thoughts and beliefs. I think it is to do with self-hypnotisation as well. We all have some similar saying, "Words cut more than swords." That simply can represent how powerful words can be.'

In an attempt to see just how strong harsh words can be, IKEA United Arab Emirates partnered with media company Memac Ogilvy to create an anti-bullying campaign featuring plants. A group of schoolchildren were asked to 'bully' one plant and use positive language to another, and their insults were recorded. After a month, the bullied plant appeared to have wilted, while the complimented plant was healthy. Although these results were met with a mixed response, it at the very least illustrates our belief that words can affect living organisms.

After a series of experiments, Japanese author and doctor of alternative medicine Masaru Emoto, who has a small but ardent following in Japan, claimed that the molecular structure of water transforms when exposed to human words. Although his work is largely considered to be pseudoscience or even a 'cult', his proposition is an interesting one to consider and an example of how some people still believe in the power *kotodama*. In his book *The Hidden Messages in Water*, Emoto mentions a study of the Fujiwara Dam, which purportedly saw a significant change after a Shinto priest repeated incantations there.

Whatever your take on these investigations, it would seem that the power of speech or words is universally understood to have some kind of impact on the way humans (or plants, water and cats) will behave. It's worth wondering whether cats, if they had had an inner voice, would speak badly of themselves or others? Or would their effortless confidence quell any negative projections?

I spoke to Rachel Carroll, a wellbeing coach who uses neurolinguistic programming – changing our thoughts, language and behaviour to achieve our goals – in her work as a barometer, microscope and panacea for what ails her clients. 'The words we choose and what we say to ourselves matters,' she said. 'Squashing negative self-talk is a wellbeing tool I bring into my clients' awareness very early on in our coaching sessions. Why is it we think it's okay to berate and harangue ourselves with our internal voice when there's no way we would speak to our best friend, or our cat for that matter, in such a poor way? The fact that cats do not use words to describe, define and create their worlds is to their advantage. We humans definitely limit ourselves with our words.'

She added, 'The way we speak to ourselves is important because words have power. I like that the Japanese have a word for this power, this spirit: *kotodama*. As an example of *kotodama*, the power of words, I am reminded of the first time I moved to Japan. I lived alone in a regional city called Fukuchiyama in Kyoto-fu [prefecture].

'At times early on in that first year I really struggled, just as most expats do, with the massive change and totally different way of life in Japan. Some days I felt really frustrated and depressed just at the thought of trying to mail a parcel at the post office, such a simple task, quickly and easily completed at home in Australia in my native tongue surrounded by my compatriots. But in Japan, not so. In Japan it was a protracted process, sometimes taking three times as long. The power of words in creating our world, our experience of life, is such that if I told myself the trip to the post office was a pain, a hassle and something difficult to be dreaded, then it was. If I told myself my Japanese was not good enough or I didn't know enough vocabulary to get the job done, then that was true too.

'Only, once I chose to embrace the challenge, the opportunity to grow my vocabulary and confidence speaking Japanese, then my outlook changed and so did my results posting parcels.'

Rachel concluded: 'If we are, as I believe we are, creating the world we are experiencing, then why not choose what we want to experience? Who wouldn't want to do that? Words are a human beings' way of making sense of the universe, the world we live in. Or perhaps "the *worlds* we live in" is more accurate. When it comes to defining, describing and creating our worlds, how would we be feeling if we chose only the words that light us up? Only those words that make us feel good? Words do have the power to make us feel good. Cats certainly don't seem to box themselves into invisible cages, do they?'

Cats and language

While cats lack the ability to interpret exactly what we say to them, they can pick up on our tone of voice.

Certified feline behaviourist Marilyn Krieger says, 'Cats are very sensitive and can feel safe or feel threatened by the tone of voice and the loudness. Cats are more apt to respond and socialise with their people when spoken to in a soft and calm voice.' Interesting research from a university in Tokyo also provided evidence that cats can understand their owners' voices and can distinguish between words, although they do not attach any meaning to them.

What if we could be more feline in our approach to how we respond to words and situations? Since cats are highly selective in what they hear, it's unlikely they would waste their precious time on negative self-talk or gossip like we humans do.

Kishi kaisei: coming back from the brink

An interesting Japanese idiom is *kishi kaisei*, which means to 'Wake from death and return to life' or 'To come out of a desperate situation' and is commonly used when someone is being encouraged to push on through difficult times.

Kishi kaisei is what is known in the Japanese language as a four-character compound word (*yojijukugo*), a word made up of four characters (*kanji*) and often derived from Buddhist literature. These words can have one or two definitions and can be difficult for non-Japanese speakers to understand.

Nana explains, 'The meaning of *kishi kaisei* is literal, and can be used in hospitals to refer to how the doctor brought the dying back to life or how the patient was brought back to life from dying.' She continues, 'It also means to come out of desperate situations. When you experience difficult times in life, even in English, people say "it's hell", but it's just a metaphor to mention how hard it is, not literally meaning people died and are in hell. Or people might say, "It's a new me." It doesn't mean people died. It is more like the old version of me died. It is similar to these; it is a metaphoric saying to refer to coming back from desperate situations.'

So how *do* we come back from difficult situations?

Let's use our feline friends as an example. They will likely sit with their emotions for as long as they need to rather than try to control them or obsess over them in the same way we humans tend to. As mentioned in Chapter G, if we can look upon the challenges we face in life and see them as an opportunity to transform, grow and learn, we can become more resilient.

*

Transforming adversity into something that's beneficial can take a long time and often requires help from good friends, family and a strong support network, or even different types of therapy, as well as the tenacity to keep at it. But much like the felines from Fukushima's exclusion zone, if we can open our heart again, and talk positively as well as mindfully in the spirit of *kotodama*, eventually we'll make it through.

Unmei 運命
Destiny

If you've ever had a cat, did you find them or did they find you? Could your relationship be considered fate, destiny or perhaps even karmic? And what is it that describes these cosmic chains of events? While some consider fate or destiny as nothing more than the sum of their decisions, others view these unexplained coincidences in a more spiritual light.

According to an ancient Japanese tale, people are often connected to others by an invisible red thread that binds them together, and those ties can never be broken. In East Asian culture, these ties are associated with those who are destined to meet one another and find their true love. As the Japanese proverb goes, 'Even the stone you trip on is part of your destiny.'

Whether you believe that nothing happens by chance and what unfolds is predetermined, or that serendipitous events are just a collection of coincidences, the question of fate is something many of us contemplate. In Japanese, *unmei* is a noun meaning 'fate' or 'destiny'. It's worth pointing out that in English, 'fate' can have both positive and negative connotations, whereas 'destiny' is almost exclusively positive. Some consider 'fate' to mean 'divinely planned' or something in which we can't intervene, whereas 'destiny' is often tied to a higher purpose, such as something we are meant to do and have the power to shape. In Japan, the word *unmei* can be used to describe any outcome that transcends human willpower, or something that happens irrespective of the actions we take, and can bring either happiness or misfortune depending on the context.

When I first went to Japan, I could have benefited from having more faith in my own *unmei* as I arrived as a teacher in the hilltop city of Takayama. Alas, back then all I could think was that I'd made a terrible mistake, as I struggled with the new food, language and unfamiliar culture, and tirelessly pushed against the incongruous course curriculum and daily timetable. Yet this journey led me to where I am today, writing books about cats and Japan. Whether that was a happy coincidence, some pre-written destiny, or even a reward for enduring life's lessons, I can never be too sure, but it does serve as a reminder that sometimes it's okay to allow things to unfold as they should and avoid the stress of seeking ultimate control, because perhaps what is, was always meant to be.

Cats and *unmei*

There have been countless stories all over the world of cats showing up at exactly the right time and helping when someone or something is in need. The railway cats of Diorama Restaurant Osaka, for example, are credited with saving the business when it was about to close because of the Covid pandemic. The struggling model-train-themed restaurant, opened by Naoki Teraoka in 2018, was given a new lease of life when the owner started posting images to the business's Instagram account showing his rescued stray cat and its family towering over the model railway and resting next to the tiny stations. The Godzilla-like kitties received attention from around the world, and the owner now repays the cats for saving his business by helping to rehome others like them.

There are plenty of other tales in Japan of felines saving people, businesses, stations or temples. Among some of the most popular are Tama the Station Cat, who saved a train line, or the felines connected with *neko-dera* (the nickname given to temples with a cat connection), such as Shōnen-ji Temple in Kyoto, which is famous for the folktale of a cat that brought about its reconstruction.

It might seem far-fetched, but finding my Japanese kitten outside a temple in Takayama was for me a moment that changed the course of my life significantly. If I hadn't been at that place, on that day, at that time, I wouldn't have rescued the kitten, and I would have left Japan after only a year, and I certainly wouldn't have formed the friendships I made there, got involved with the Japanese animal charity ArkBark, or even thought about writing a book about travelling with pets. Yet all these seemingly unconnected events have led me to where I am today.

Someone else whose life was affected by the intervention of a feline companion was fellow animal lover, and pet business owner, Ayami Golledge. Ayami's first cat was a black rescue called Kiwi, which coincidentally was the same for me. As a child, my first adopted cat was also a black rescue kitty named Kiwi. Our serendipitous connection prompted me to speak to her about how our destiny shapes us and what part we play in everything.

Originally from Kanagawa, Japan, Ayami Golledge has lived in several countries and now calls Melbourne home. She runs a pet business where people can take their dogs punting on the Royal Botanic Gardens lake, Cambridge-style. She had never had cats while she lived in Japan, but when she moved to New Zealand, she adopted Kiwi. Ayami said, 'Kiwi really supported me when we had numerous earthquakes in NZ. She was scared of people but not me, and I knew when she was calm that I was safe, because when we had a bad or big earthquake, she would run away.' When I asked Ayami if she thought cats choose us or we choose them, and what part fate plays in finding each other, she said, 'I think it happens both ways – we somehow attract each other! We've been looking for our rescue dog for more than one and a half years actually but no luck yet, but we'll wait for our destiny.' She added, 'Since ancient times, people have thought cats are good luck because they take mice (who are considered to be bad luck) away.'

Regarding the legend of the invisible red string of destiny that binds people together, Ayami explained, 'In Japan, sometimes people believe that things are meant to happen. The word *akai-ito* or "red string" is normally used for a man and woman, and lots of people in Japan use this expression when you find the right partner. According to this myth, the gods tie an invisible red string around the ankles of men and women who are destined to be soul mates and will one day marry each other. People often say *Unmei no akai-ito*, which means "red string of destiny". *Akai-ito* is used for a man and woman and the word *unmei* can be used for any sort of destiny/fate.'

Jun Tagami from Inner Nature said of the red string of fate: 'The first thing that came to my mind when I heard the words "red string" was from the *Hannya Shingyo*

[Heart Sutra].' He continued, 'What this is saying is that each of us is supported by countless lives to exist here and now. Not only our ancestors, but also the people we meet, birds, dogs, cats, all living creatures, micro-organisms, plants, cars, books, beds and other materials, and the mental world of thoughts and memories are all involved as life. And all of them form the universe. Without the universe we would not exist, but conversely the universe would not exist without us. I thought this is *engi* [which describes the relationship between cause and effect] and the true nature of the ultimate red thread.'

Interpretations of the Heart Sutra can vary slightly from person to person, culture to culture or in different Buddhist lineages. The Heart Sutra is well known in Japan and teaches the concept of *kū* (voidness), or the emptiness of every being and every object, impermanence and how everything is interdependent, not separate or in isolation. This is reminiscent of the cause-and-effect principles in the teachings of karma.

Cats and karma

When it comes to cats and evaluating the sum of their actions, many people find it interesting to ponder whether their intentions are pure or if they are simply being manipulative. People often say, 'Cats don't love you, they just use you,' or 'Cats have no loyalty, they'll go wherever there's food.' But as they snuggle up with you on the couch, purring delightfully as you pet them, it's hard to believe they're displaying anything other than reciprocated love.

In the anthology *The Karma of Cats*, editor Diana Ventimiglia and the other authors credit cats with being spiritual teachers. During the introduction, humanitarian activist Seane Corn says that when a cat comes to us, we establish a karmic bond.

Much like the hero kitties saving businesses and temples; or Ayami's sweet cat, Kiwi, who helped her to settle into a new life in New Zealand; or my own Takayama rescue who changed my life in Japan, cats, Corn explains, 'show up in our little human worlds to teach us essential life lessons. And if we allow these lessons to permeate our awareness, they will change who we are, and we will be better for it.'

While many of us have heard the word 'karma' before, its true meaning is often missed. It's often mistakenly categorised with sayings such as 'What goes around comes around' or 'An eye for an eye', suggesting that karma is sort of like Santa Claus, dishing out gifts to the good and lumps of coal to the bad. In reality, karma is less about being rewarded or punished, and more about developing a deeper sense of mindfulness in our actions so that we can take agency and responsibility for what's going on around us.

When I asked Venerable Rinchen Kelly from the Khacho Yulo Ling Buddhist Centre to explain the meaning of 'karma' and how it is connected to fate, she said, 'Karma is not predestined, and therefore things can only change depending on your intention rather than fate or destiny. If your intention is mundane, then the result will be mundane. For example, if you win $100,000 and decide to donate the money to a worthy charity, but on the way to the bank you suffer from a moment of miserly nature and decide to give significantly less, then the karmic result for you will be far less.'

But what do we mean by 'karmic result'?

To understand this, we need to be aware that every time we make a choice, we change the course of both our lives and the lives of those around us. For each action we take, there will be a corresponding reaction, much like how skimming pebbles on a still lake will not only cause the stone to move but will also cause the water to ripple. This 'ripple effect', as some people have come to understand it, is at the heart of the teachings of karma. It suggests that nothing is coincidental; rather, seeds have been planted in a previous life, and we have the opportunity to grow something positive in the world if we set the right intentions and practise generosity.

In the words of one Buddhist spiritual teacher, 'Karma moves in two directions. If we act virtuously, the seed we plant will result in happiness. If we act non-virtuously, suffering results.'

Synchronicity

On the other hand, 'synchronicity', a term coined by Swiss psychoanalyst Carl Jung, is used to explain things that couldn't necessarily be explained by cause and effect alone, such as a chance meeting with someone you know in a faraway land, talking of something and it coincidentally materialising, or perhaps a cat showing up in your garden the same colour as the one you had previously dreamt about. Many experts suggest that these 'recognisable patterns' might be due to people seeking them out, perhaps due to a traumatic event triggering the individual to look out for these so-called signs.

One of the main differences between karma and synchronicity is that karma makes us fully responsible for what we do either in this life or the next, but if we were to solely rely on the notion of synchronicity we would have no responsibility for the self. For many people, however, heeding signs from the universe is a proactive way of managing one's destiny.

Yuriko Sato, a Japanese Jungian psychoanalyst and psychotherapist based in Zurich, presented a talk titled *Synchronicity: A Common Reality in Japan* at the Pari Center in Switzerland. She spoke about how her maternal grandfather experienced two similar synchronistic events. The first was when he received a message with an image of a sinking ship from a fortune paper at a temple. Her grandfather worked for a shipping company, and so he called his wife who in turn relayed that one of the company's ships had indeed sunk. The second example involved planning which job to take, one in Hiroshima or one in Kyoto. Both were similar and equal in opportunity, so he consulted the *i-ching* (an ancient Chinese text used for divination), which instructed him not to accept the job in Hiroshima otherwise 'he would die'. This was just before the tragic atomic bombing of the city in August 1945.

Yuriko also highlights the importance of dreams in Japanese culture, and how most people share some level of belief in the invisible world, which she explains using the Shinto belief in *kami* (divine spirits) as well as the Hua-yen Buddhist view (or *Kegon*, as it's known in Japan) of interdependence or oneness. She refers to a Korean documentary that discusses how Easterners and Westerners see the world differently. The documentary illustrated this point with a ball: in the West it's seen as an object in empty space; whereas in the East it's thought to be viewed as being surrounded by energy (or *chi*), indicating that there's something beyond what one sees. Of course, Yuriko is careful to clarify that the definitions between East and West are not so clear in today's rapidly globalised world, but regardless of our individual traditions, drawing upon this Eastern way of viewing the world could help us find more meaning in life, give us hope in the impossible, and provide a type of reassurance that things will turn out how they were meant to.

If you can trust in the unfolding fate of your life, you are likely to become more aware of synchronicity. Carl Jung once said, 'Synchronicity is an ever-present reality for those who have eyes to see it.' This suggests that we all have the ability to tap in to this magic but too often choose not to, when we are too wrapped-up in our egos or the material world. If it sometimes feels as if fate is working against you, then it could be that having limited knowledge of the future and an incessant need for control is blinding you from something better. What if instead of trying to ruin your life, fate is simply trying to bring your attention towards a different path and redirect you to where you're supposed to be, not where you think you should be?

Whether you believe in karma or synchronicity is of course entirely up to you, and both may seem relevant at different times in your life. But it is also worth considering the importance of the Buddhist approach of creating the right karmic conditions. By practising compassion to all sentient beings unselfishly, we can make the world a kinder place.

Shinto snakes

Before arriving in Japan, most people would have probably described me as somewhat of a sceptic. I didn't pay much attention to so-called signs and would most likely write things like that off as being all a bit 'woo-woo', but as my time in Japan passed, the people and the cats there showed me that sometimes what might seem impossible could be possible. I learned that unless you are open, you might struggle to find the right path. In the end, the things you end up with might not be the ones you exactly wished for – but who knows, they may end up being even better.

In Shintoism, snakes are considered very sacred animals. For example, having snakeskin in your wallet is believed to bring prosperity and luck, so snakeskin wallets are quite common in Japan. One morning, in a conversation with a friend about the difficult decision to quit my current job, pack up and move again, we talked about the similarity between the transformational nature of relocation and a snake shedding its skin. As soon as our conversation ended, I decided to research the significance of snakes in Japanese culture. Just as snakes shed their skin when they outgrow it, when we move house we change not just our belongings but part of our former selves. As I stared at the phone screen waiting for the results to load, I heard a commotion between two large crows noisily bashing about in the bush beside me. Startled, I stopped looking at my phone and turned to see what was behind me. About a metre away a long green tree snake slithered across the footpath. What was the meaning behind this eery presence? Was the universe trying to grab my attention? Was this synchronicity in action? Or was it merely coincidence?

I then learned that in Japan snakes are considered so auspicious that many people keep a snakeskin in a box or hang it from the rafters for good luck. The timing was not lost on me, and prompted me to investigate further. Was I, as Jung would likely suggest, seeking recognisable patterns in the upheaval of a forthcoming move and impending surgery?

I could write off the uncanny timing of seeing a snake while I was searching for their significance as just a fluke, and I'm sure the old me would have done so, but could it be, as some suggest, that the more engaged we become spiritually, the more these types of things occur? Whatever you may think of synchronistic events, if they happen often enough they're difficult to ignore and can feel like magic. If we view these events with an open mind and resist the tendency to shrug them off as merely coincidental, we might begin to attract more such moments that we can use to learn or grow.

Allowing the magic in

We seem to spend so much time telling ourselves what we don't want rather than what we do. We don't want to work late, go to the gym or eat too much chocolate, and that leaves very little room for anything else. What if you could change the conversation and leave some room for some magic to manifest? In the spirit of *kotodama*, as we saw in the previous chapter, if we try using words that tell a different story, would the things we wish for come true? I'm not talking about winning the lottery (although that might be nice) but about achievable goals: the job you'd like to get, the holiday you wish to take, or the cat you'd like to welcome into your family. Perhaps, if we can remove our ego from the situation, and our need to control, we might allow for more of the good stuff to creep in. But as Venerable Rinchen said, planting the seeds with the right intention will create the right karmic conditions, so we must not do this in a selfish way, but for the benefit of all beings.

It's good to have curiosity and be inquisitive – what the Japanese would call *shoshin* or a 'beginner's mind', a concept from Zen Buddhism. After all, if we don't follow the hints we're given, we might miss something truly wonderful. It may be a homeless silver kitten next to a temple or something else entirely, but this type of synchronicity doesn't come from the internet; it comes from being outside in the world, talking with people face to face, and being in situations that are sometimes unknown or unfamiliar.

While life might be what we make it – through positive thinking, taking time to notice (what some might call expanded awareness or the Samurai state), or the power of words – that doesn't always mean it goes according to plan. Although the concept of *unmei* is certainly enticing, we have to be aware that some things are beyond our control, and accept that if something isn't going right we can't make it so – like the cat that wants to climb the tree and ends up getting stuck. What we can do is lay the groundwork for positive changes in our life by being more open, nurturing the right seeds, and considering that where we are right now might actually be where we need to be.

Positive changes to impact your *unmei*

1. **Talk to people who are different from you** – Variety is the spice of life. While this might sound daunting if you are shy or introverted, you may miss out on many interactions with truly amazing people if you shut yourself off. It's by opening up that we allow more opportunities to flow in. Speak to your local shopkeeper, the person next to you on the train, or the person you see on your daily walk.

2. **Reduce your time online** – Synchronicities and creating good karma won't happen if you're stuck at home on your own. Don't let these incidents of spiritual significance pass you by because you're glued to a computer screen.

3. **Join a group in person** – Be part of a community, ask questions and go deeper. For those of us who are introverted, joining a new group is a challenge but the rewards are worth it. Remember, you are probably not the only introvert in the group and will likely find other people with whom you have lots in common.

4. **Do a good deed and practise generosity** – Plant your karmic seeds, help others and yourself. Heal the negative

karma by knowing the decisions you make now can affect your future.

5. **Unlock your dreams** – Ask the universe for signs, create a vision board, do oracle cards, write a list of things you want to happen in one year, five years or ten years. Put your goals out there and see what happens (just make sure your intentions are good).

Wabi-sabi 侘び寂び
Imperfectly perfect

Beauty can emerge in the unlikeliest of places, such as the charm of a decaying old ramshackle cottage, the greying whiskers of an ageing cat, or the weathered face of a raggedy toy a furry friend once loved so dearly. In Japanese aesthetics, *wabi-sabi* encompasses this very sentiment, encouraging us to embrace the natural ageing elements that exist around us. It is an appreciation for the stories told in every imperfection and the novelty of each transition, and an acceptance that nothing is truly complete. To experience *wabi-sabi*, we can look in a variety of places, from the dynamic transformation of flora throughout the seasons, to the dog-eared creases of a beloved book.

While the Western view of beauty typically places emphasis on perfection, youth and symmetry, Japanese aesthetics are much more complex. Rooted in ancient philosophy, Japanese aesthetics favour the transient and unfinished over that which stands proudly in full bloom. In this way, something that is slightly broken or flawed is not looked upon as damaged or ruined, but instead the more beautiful for it.

Although there is no English translation for the term *wabi-sabi*, and it is difficult to explain, put simply it's about finding beauty within the imperfections of life. During my research for this book, it quickly became apparent that *wabi-sabi* has different connotations for different people, so I have included some examples to illustrate. For example, Ayami Golledge, from whom we heard in the previous chapter, describes *wabi-sabi* as 'Finding beauty in simple and quiet [peaceful] and incomplete things. Japanese people sometimes find more beauty in imperfect or incomplete things.' She adds, '*Wabi* is beauty coming from simplicity, while *sabi* is beauty or serenity that comes with age.' Tokyo-based artist Chie Tokuyama gave a slightly different take, explaining, '*Wabi-sabi* could be thought of as the ageing of humans themselves. Our physical appearance and mentality change with age, which makes us have diverse minds and unique features – even our wrinkles carry knowledge and history. I always try to express *wabi-sabi* in my paintings.'

Over the course of this book, we have so far considered six of the seven main principles for achieving *wabi-sabi*: *datsuzoku* (break from routine), *fukinsei* (letting go of concepts), *kanso* (simplicity), *kokō* (austerity), *seijaku* (stillness and tranquillity), and *shizen* (naturalness). In the next chapter, we'll dive into the last of these seven principles with *yūgen* (ethereal beauty), but for now let's consider the origins of *wabi-sabi* in more depth.

The history of *wabi-sabi* and the tea ceremony

The Japanese tea ceremony is known as *sadō* or *chadō* (the way of tea) or *chanoyu* (hot water for tea) and has its roots in Zen Buddhism. The ritualistic traditions of the Japanese tea ceremony teach the importance of purity, simplicity and finding perfection in the imperfect, while also illuminating the idea that nothing is perfect.

Ritual tea drinking began in China and was first performed in Japan during the Kamakura period (1192–1333) by Zen monks, who drank tea to alleviate tiredness during long sessions of meditation. But as tea ceremonies gradually became less focused on simplicity and more on luxury, when warlords and shōguns began to use the ritual to show off their power and strength, the ceremony became unmoored from its humble beginnings.

The Zen priests who encouraged the return of the spiritual element of the tea ceremony were Ikkyū (1394–1481), a monk and poet, and then his student

Jukō Murata (1423–1502, also written Shukō Murata). A Zen priest, Murata proposed a move from the distractions of expensive decorative cups and luxury towards a more minimalist approach, and began to develop the *wabi-cha* style of tea ceremony, which favoured simplicity over splendour. Murata's most notable document is a letter called *Kokoro no fumi* (*Letter of the Heart*), which expresses a desire to 'harmonise Japanese and Chinese tastes', as well as a dislike for others' excessive concern with the imperfections and rustic aesthetics of Japanese utensils. Following the death of Murata, his successor, Jōō Takeno (1502–55), continued to develop the *wabi-cha* style, but it was Takeno's pupil, Sen no Rikyū (1522–91), who was responsible for perfecting this most treasured tradition.

I spoke with Mayumi Kojima, a naturopath and Japanese tea ceremony enthusiast who holds regular workshops on different aspects of Japanese culture, to find out more about the history of *wabi-sabi* and its connection to the tea ceremony. She explained: 'The *wabi-sabi* concept was started from Taoism during the [Chinese] Song Dynasty (960–1279) and much later influenced Zen Buddhist teachings around the mid-sixteenth century. This was around the same time as the tea ceremony became popular in Japan, and the *wabi-sabi* style of tea ceremony was particularly regarded amongst powerful influencers of the time, such as Sen no Rikyū, as well as tea masters and feudal lords such as Nobunaga

Oda and Hideyoshi Toyotomi. *Wabi-sabi* was originally seen as an ascetic and modest way of appreciating and admiring beauty.'

Speaking of the great tea master Sen no Rikyū, she added, 'I believe that *wabi-sabi* is the way to describe life, death and its beauty.' Sen no Rikyū preached and transcended life and death throughout his life with his tea ceremony practice.

If you have ever attended a tea ceremony, you will no doubt have noticed how it automatically makes you more observant; you simply couldn't enjoy it if you were in a rushed or heightened state. It is the perfect opportunity to block out the busyness of the outside world. The purposeful movements, careful attention to detail, Zen-like precision of where the pots are placed, how the cloth is folded, how the tea is stirred, and how everything is delivered in a certain order are characteristic of the ceremony, causing you to automatically slow down. Turning the teacup or bowl to make sure the correct side is given to the guest, who then returns this respect by turning the teacup back for the host when they've finished, acts as a way to honour one another. At its heart is *kissako*, which means 'drink tea, leave' and comes from the Buddhist idea that Zen is not divorced from the ordinary process of life.

When I asked Mayumi to explain this concept a little more, she said, '*Kissako*, in Buddhist teaching, is to eliminate segregation. It teaches us to treat everyone equally without assumption, by offering tea to each person. It doesn't matter where they come from, or when they appear to us, we must serve them without judgement, maintaining the same level of hospitality and dignity, being modest and humble, always applying ourselves the best on any occasion.'

Cats and *ichi-go ichi-e*

Wabi-sabi allows us to enjoy the tea ceremony in its purest form, free of distractions, but another important philosophy at the heart of this tradition is *ichi-go ichi-e* ('one chance in a lifetime'), which teaches that every meeting is special and cannot be repeated. As we saw in Chapter N, *ichi-go ichi-e* is an idiom that can be traced back to sixteenth-century Japan. It was created by Sōji Yamanoue, a senior disciple of Sen no Rikyū. According to Mayumi, the original meaning was to highlight that 'every tea ceremony is a once-in-a-lifetime event'. It's a lesson in appreciating the moment as it comes because it's the only time you'll get to experience it.

Cats are the embodiment of appreciating the moment, and can teach us a lot about the value of *ichi-go ichi-e*. These creatures are constantly content to enjoy life as it comes, unburdened by dreams of the future or wistful longing for the past. They don't dread the inevitable ageing process or run around hectically trying to juggle various tasks.

When I asked Mayumi her opinion on whether cats have the ability to experience *ichi-go ichi-e*, she replied, 'I personally think they do. Any occasion can be seen like that, if we choose to see it that way. The moments I spend time with a person or even my cat, Milky Boy, will never ever be repeated again. I can't bring time with my cat back, whether it is good times or bad times.'

She added, 'I always try to remind myself that Milky Boy is getting older, and I was told by the vet that he only has six months to live. Spending time with him has given me so much joy; he even makes me feel better when I am having a bad day. He appeared in my life almost twenty years ago, with a skinny face; his ears were so dirty. I could tell that he was wandering for a while – maybe he was looking for his original owner. I called YAPS [an animal refuge near Cairns] and the RSPCA but I was secretly hoping that no one would claim him. And the rest is history.'

Talking of their relationship, Mayumi said, 'We made such a special friendship. He was in my life when I was going through a tough time, like my depression through my marriage, health challenges and all of that. Some people may say "He's just a cat", and he is a cat but he's not "just a cat". He taught me in a way what *ichi-go ichi-e* is, that each day is precious and a miracle. Even just cuddling him and hearing his purr is so special to me, knowing that someday we will say goodbye to each other. That is why I treasure each moment with him, not hesitating to say I love him, and thank Milky Boy every day. I think it is very *ichi-go ichi-e*!'

Cats and *wabi-sabi*

So far in this chapter, we have discussed how the Japanese Aesthetic Principles of *wabi-sabi* can encourage us to value the simple things in life such as the sound of a cat purring in the morning, or the beautiful grey streaks across a cat's ageing face. By slowing down and accepting that impermanence is an inevitable part of life, we can bring our attention back to the present and try to enjoy each moment more mindfully as we embrace the teachings of *ichi-go ichi-e*.

If we study our feline friends, we will see that they embody many of these Japanese concepts and show us that it's not always necessary to strive for more, show off or live excessively, but instead to find peace with just enough. They say cats see the world through shades of blue and green, but I think their view on life is probably a technicolour dream. Without wasting unnecessary energy overcomplicating each moment, cats maintain a simple yet peaceful outlook on life with no constant cravings (unless there are treats around). Cats are connoisseurs of slow-paced living, appreciating life's normally unappreciated subtleties, like a cosy spot on top of the radiator, a pile of fresh laundry or a warm meal.

Incomplete perfection

The sentiments of *wabi-sabi* have been appreciated for centuries and are still relevant today. *Wabi-sabi* can help us to make peace with ourselves as we alter our preconceptions around perfection, appreciate that nothing lasts forever, and make the most of each moment. As my friend Rachel once said, life is like those vintage slide tile puzzles, which can only become complete in the absence of a particular piece. Rachel said, 'You need to be able to slide the tiles around inside the frame to make the picture. If there was not a missing piece, then you couldn't move any of the tiles. You'd be stuck with what you've got. The presence of an empty space creates the room required to slide the other tiles around to complete the picture. You cannot solve the puzzle unless there is that missing tile to facilitate movement towards the wholeness of the picture. So the slide tile puzzles speak to the acceptance of the nature of our existence: nothing is perfect, there is always a tile missing, but that doesn't mean our life is incomplete or broken. In the case of the slide tile puzzles, the missing piece is the very component that completes them.'

It can be hard to stop obsessing over the need to complete everything until it's perfect, especially when this type of messaging is so rife in modern society. To see incompleteness as opportunity for further growth, or to view the scars of your past as something to wear with pride instead of shame, could help you find peace in the present. It's these imperfections that tell the stories of our life, and the missing pieces hold all of our potential for change.

For example, I used to view the derelict West Pier in Brighton, Sussex, on England's south coast very differently from how I see it now. In the past, I saw it as an ugly, neglected eyesore, but today can appreciate its withering decay, its juxtaposition with the skyline, the starling murmurations that swoop around it, and how it stands proudly in the ocean with all of its scars, in contrast to the shiny new i360, a 162-metre-high observation tower that many of the locals (including my friend Sophie) dislike. Shigeo Kondo-Maher, the former Paris syndrome sufferer from whom we heard from in Chapter P, and now a resident of Sussex, said, 'As someone who comes from Kyoto I can sympathise with the old West Pier. Perhaps as Brighton is the capital of hipsters, the local authority really understood about *wabi-sabi*.'

*

Like the great tea masters Sen no Rikyū, Murata and Ikkyū, who each developed elements of *wabi-sabi* in relation to the tea ceremony, we too can acknowledge the natural cycle of growth and decay. After all, most things become chipped and rusted over time – it's an inevitable part of life. Perhaps instead of fearing time or trying to control it, we can use these teachings as a reminder to accept the incompleteness of life and age more gracefully.

Yūgen 幽玄
Ethereal beauty

Cats can leave us lost for words. Whether we are awestruck by their beauty or aghast by their behaviour, we often find ourselves unable to express how we feel.

Yūgen, the seventh and final Japanese principle of *wabi-sabi* for us to consider, is one of the most important Japanese aesthetic concepts. Employed in poetry and other forms of art, especially from the Middle Ages, its definition is somewhat elusive as it varies depending on the period, person or work, but it's usually described as mysterious profundity, ethereal beauty or the subtle grace of the universe. While the direct translation may depend on the context, the most common explanation of *yūgen* is 'an awareness of the universe that triggers emotional responses too deep and powerful for words'.

Yū means 'faint' or 'dim', while *gen* means 'profound reason', or subtle and mysterious circumstances that are hidden in the essence of things and are not easily known. Writer Andrew R. Deane said, 'There is an obvious and intimate connection between Zen and *yūgen*, as both are concerned with "the true nature of reality that hides behind the illusory aspects of the world".' Picture the fog dancing over a mountain sunrise in pristine wilderness, or the half-light at dusk over a shipwreck on the ocean. It's the suggestion that is created and your response to it that sums up the beauty of *yūgen*.

Experiencing *yūgen*

Dark-blue and greenish-yellow lights dashed across the window as I stared out into the dark abyss. I was captivated by what I saw. Standing next to me onboard a night flight to Tokyo was a Japanese gentleman who had been busy telling me about his visit to the Sigmund Freud Museum in London when we were both suddenly dazzled by the bright lights of the Aurora Borealis. This man, Yūzo Takei, also happened to be an expert in meteorology, and a retired colonel of the Japan Air Self-Defense Force. As we admired nature's dancing light display, I asked him to explain more about *yūgen* – this most Japanese of concepts. He said, 'For me, *yūgen* is an is expression of atmosphere, such as a powerful spot, one that exists at a forest shrine, or a holy site in the deep mountainous region far away from anything – where no one lives, like a mythological world, or the mysterious air of the faint dark.'

With this I learned that *yūgen* is not just about seeing something beautiful in nature, it is more about the feeling you get when you experience something that is subtle and profound. It can also be described as the sensation of experiencing it, or as Yūzo Takei described it, as 'atmosphere'. Like the unseen beauty of what lies beneath the traditional *torii* gate as you look out over the serene waters of an inland sea or the steep winding steps that lead up to a remote temple. It brings about an emotional response that is difficult to describe, and can make you aware of how small you are in the universe.

Yūgen is core to Noh theatre, a classical Japanese dance-drama that has been performed since the fourteenth century. Izumi Purnell, a Japanese remedial yoga instructor, studied Japanese classical literature at Waseda University in Tokyo, including Noh theatre. Izumi-san has a traditional take on *yūgen*, one that is deeply connected to its interpretation by Zeami Motokiyo, a Japanese aesthetician, actor and playwright who, together with his father, was responsible for developing the Noh drama in its present form to be performed at temples and shrines in Japan. Izumi-san says, 'For me, *yūgen* is so deep that it goes beyond description, something that's hard to know, hard to be sure. For example, the beauty of a Noh face mask, the change of expression depending on the subtle angle of the face, and the underlying inescapable sadness of being human.'

Izumi-san's graduation thesis was a comparison of Zeami's theatrical literature and Shakespeare's plays. It mainly focused on the sorrows, sufferings and psychological madness of human beings, which were expressed through the works of both writers. She adds, 'I also practised Noh dance and singing as a student, with a master who represented a family of Shimogakari Hōshō-ryū, the professional Noh actors.'

Regarding Zeami Motokiyo and the concept of *yūgen*, she says, 'He made a great interpretation of it and deepened, broadened or narrowed the meaning. I found the modern way of adapting the word *yūgen*, especially in English-speaking society, is a little too light physically. I would never use the word to describe a mystical connection with the universe or nature during bright daylight. It has to be maybe a misty morning, twilight or sunset – darkness deepens the mysterious shadows – or at night, with only the fire or moonlight showing the scenery or someone's face or expressions, you cannot see clearly. From my understanding, in Zeami's time the world was so much darker, with only a bit of candlelight. Hence in Japan, if you go to Noh outdoor theatre, which is called Takigi Noh, it's only lit up by wooden fire torches. The shadow and darkness are a very important part of the beauty of *yūgen*.'

These words of Zeami Motokiyo, famous in Japan, characterise the meaning of *yūgen*:

> To watch the sun sink behind a flower-clad hill. To wander on in a huge forest without thought of return. To stand upon the shore and gaze after a boat that disappears behind distant islands. To contemplate the flight of wild geese seen and lost among the clouds. And subtle shadows of bamboo on bamboo.

Izumi-san says, 'It implies the sadness of the sun setting combined with the short life of flowers, expressing the awareness of impermanence. I think Zeami's *yūgen* was adopted from the feeling of *mono no aware*, which was one of the most expressed feelings in *Genji Monogatari* [known in the West as *The Tale of Genji*] from the Heian period – the acute awareness of impermanence of human life.'

Izumi-san stresses that *yūgen* is more than just being awed by nature and the universe, as is often implied by some sources: 'For me, *yūgen* is not really talking about the awesomeness of nature but more about human sentiments. The deeper sentiments, which cannot be expressed now or ever, however, can be felt. It is seeping through beyond obvious physical expressions, and it can be felt through the impermanent beauty in nature, like a sunset, change of seasons, end of a flower blooming, tree leaves falling. Nothing stays the same forever; the awareness of impermanence adds to the beauty of nature itself. The feeling of *yūgen* doesn't exist without humans witnessing it.'

When we discuss what *yūgen* can teach us, she says, 'The beauty and depth of it are not always or necessarily obviously expressed physically and verbally. It could be hidden; however, it can be felt by quieting our mind and paying closer attention to small details in life and nature. In Zeami's plays, if you become oversensitive or too clinging, obsessed with these feelings, you can go crazy, you can lose your mind in the mystery of it.'

Cats and *yūgen*

Could the relationship between cat and human be considered *yūgen*?

The profound connection between human and animal can trigger a response too powerful for words – the way they know exactly what to do when we're in need; the way they seem to find us at our lowest point; or how they're able to forge such powerful silent relationships with a different species while retaining their wild essence. Cats can make us believe in a deep, cosmic interconnectedness of all living things because of their innate capacity to weave seamlessly into our lives.

When I consider Izumi-san's examination of *yūgen* – that it's not just about the awesomeness of nature, but more about human sentiments – I'm reminded that all relationships between humans and animals are by their very nature impermanent. As Izumi-san says, 'nothing stays the same forever.' We live with our cats knowing full well we'll have to say goodbye to them one day. We'll probably have to make a call on their life, or hold them as they go. For me, that feeling – that intense love inexorably linked to such great sadness – can be thought of as *yūgen*.

Our feline friends don't just amaze us with their elegant beauty and fantastic feats, they can also use their abilities to care for us. For example, because of their exceptional sense of smell, cats can tell if their human is sick, detecting small chemical and hormonal changes within their owner's body. Another skill that strengthens our cat–human bond is their potential to tell when we are coming home, so that they can run to meet us with their tails up when the front door opens. Have you ever been really upset and noticed the furry presence of a feline curling up beside you just at the right time? Many people admire this intuitive nature of cats, and believe it reveals a sixth sense that allows them to pick up on things we can't, such as cancer, environmental dangers, and even the supernatural.

Since ancient times cats have been revered for their mystical powers, from the Pharaoh-protecting felines of Ancient Egypt to the pampered pets of Imperial Japan. These enigmatic creatures have a long history in Japan, appearing in Japanese folklore, literature and artwork, and are said to have special powers associated with helping people and bringing good fortune. This well-established fascination with the awesomeness of cats can be traced back centuries to Japanese royalty. On 11 March 889 CE, seventeen-year-old Emperor Uda praised his cat in his diary called *The Kanpyō Gyoki*, writing:

The colour of the fur is peerless. None could find the words to describe it, although one said it was reminiscent of the deepest ink. It has an air about it, similar to Kanno. Its length is 5 sun [15 centimetres], and its height is 6 sun [18 centimetres]. I affixed a bow about its neck, but it did not remain for long.

In rebellion, it narrows its eyes and extends its needles. It shows its back.

When it lies down, it curls in a circle like a coin. You cannot see its feet. It's as if it were a circular Bi [jade] disk. When it stands, its cry expresses profound loneliness, like a black dragon floating above the clouds.

By nature, it likes to stalk birds. It lowers its head and works its tail. It can extend its spine to raise its height by at least 2 sun [6 centimetres]. Its colour allows it to disappear at night. I am convinced it is superior to all other cats.

The emperor's diary is reminiscent of the feelings of many modern cat owners, whose mysterious creatures have been able to move them beyond words. This might be through their physical beauty or something more peculiar, like their ability to use their whiskers to aid movement in low light, or using their heightened senses to detect changes in atmospheric pressure or predict earthquakes. One such example of this was recorded in 2018, when the resident felines at a cat cafe in Osaka were videoed acting strangely just before an earthquake hit the city. While scientific data on this may vary, it's just another wondrous mystery of our feline friends.

Unusual animal behaviours are described as 'important phenomena' and are being researched around the world. One Japanese study looked at the unusual behaviour in cats and dogs before an earthquake, and found that due to their 'superior senses, dogs and cats show a greater sensitivity to small changes in smell and/or sound in their environment than humans'. Researchers have suggested that 'animals might respond to massive amounts of positive airborne ions, massive amounts of toxic gases and electromagnetic waves of ultralow and extremely low frequency'. Others have suggested that cats have a special sensitivity to the Earth's magnetic fields. The reasons aren't completely clear and may remain so.

Why is *yūgen* important?

In a world where logic, digitalisation and convenience are seemingly revered over unknowable, enigmatic conundrums, there is little room for mystery anymore – if we are uncertain of something we can always ask Google or get an app for it. But what if it's good for us to not know the answer to everything and instead savour the mystery? Depths of possibility lie in the potential to suspend our disbelief and be amazed by something indefinable. Sometimes, by trying to make sense of everything we can limit our understanding, but when we are open we become more receptive to the infinite possibilities that exist.

While fear of the unknown is normal, it can prevent us from exploring the wider world, but if we find the courage to stray from our normal boundaries and routines, we can learn more about ourselves and what we're truly capable of. Like us, cats prefer the safety and comfort of the familiar, yet every now and then something will get the better of our kitties and they'll be lured by an insatiable desire to go beyond what they know. As the saying goes, 'Curiosity killed the cat but satisfaction brought it back.' It's in these times of being pushed beyond our comfort zone that growth occurs and exciting and transcendent moments take place. The mystery of *yūgen* teaches us how small we are in relation to the universe, and that to achieve our full potential we sometimes need to push ourselves beyond the normal. After all, we're not likely to experience the indefinable in the comfort of our bedrooms.

If we look for mystery and magic in our normal life, we will open up new magical ways of seeing the world. By welcoming in the concept of *yūgen*, we will develop a new appreciation for the invisible and unexplainable. It's even been reported that experiencing awe can improve physical and mental health, possibly even lowering the risk of type 2 diabetes, clinical depression, heart disease and arthritis, according to a scientific review conducted by Berkeley University psychologists in the United States. The reported benefits were similar to those enjoyed from eating right and exercising. American writer Douglas Rushkoff says that finding awe in things is what separates us from machines, and that the sensation of being awed by nature is being gradually lost in today's society.

Experiencing *yūgen* can remind us how insignificant worrying about the trivialities of life can be. Deep down we all know that choosing what to wear at the weekend or what colour shoes to buy really isn't that important in the grand scheme of things. *Yūgen* can remind us that even though what we are experiencing might feel like the end of the world at a given time, it is largely inconsequential in the long term, which helps us put our worries in perspective. Is it worth wasting so much time and effort on that one thing that's causing you so much stress and anxiety now but probably won't have much impact on your future? Will this same issue that's keeping you awake at night still be relevant to you this time next month, let alone next year or next decade? If the answer is no, then perhaps it's best to give it less of your energy.

*

To experience the unknowable, we need to be less distracted and slow down, like your typical cat. Look around and take notice, hear the gentle pitter patter of rain on a wet day or the fluttering wings of butterflies in a garden. By embracing the teachings of *yūgen*, we can remember that even the everyday can be filled with something fascinating and unfamiliar, and once again we can view the world with a childlike wonder.

Zazen 座禅
Sitting meditation

How many times have you caught a cat sitting quietly, eyes half open, neither sleeping nor awake? It's impossible to know if they are intentionally meditating, but their serene state could still serve as an important lesson for us all. As Zen monk Shunryū Suzuki once said, 'Zen is expressed simply by sitting.'

We touched on the benefits of meditation and stillness in Chapter S, but let's look a little more deeply into *zazen*, which literally translates as 'seated meditation'. Practising *zazen* can offer us inner silence and simplicity, in stark contrast to the chaotically connected world many of us are used to. The practice and purpose of *zazen* may vary slightly between the different Zen lineages and sects, but all agree that the ultimate idea is to see the empty nature of all phenomena – including the notion of a fixed, non-changing self (ego) – and obtain enlightenment for the benefit of all beings.

It's not often that someone else will tell us to stop when things get busy, so it's our own responsibility to recognise the signs our body gives us when we need to wind down. Only we know best when it's time to rest, but unfortunately many of us regularly ignore the tell-tale signs sent from our subconscious, or find excuses that trivialise their significance, telling ourselves that we'll relax when everything is done. But since there'll always be something or someone that needs our attention, saying 'not now' and constantly putting off our much-needed rest time means we end up ignoring the one thing that really does need our attention – ourselves, here and now, in the present moment. Buddhist nun and author Kankyo Tannier suggests applying the same attention to being in the present as cats do when cleaning themselves. She writes, 'All of their concentration is focused on what they are doing in that point of time.'

I once heard someone describe meditation as being like a car sitting in neutral, and I'd always thought of it in a similar way, a stationary car with the motor running. When I asked Zen teacher Quentin Genshu of Open Way Zen about the purpose of meditation, he said, 'Meditation helps a person to control the flow of scattered thoughts in the mind and control the mind so it can become aware of what is happening in the present moment. With this calming of the activities in the mind, the mind becomes stiller and allows understanding to increase. With increasing the practice of meditation, both calmness and understanding increase, which promotes wellbeing and happiness. By increasing the amount of meditation practice, the practitioner comes to see things more clearly as they really are and this promotes a healthier body and mind.'

Since walking meditation, or *kinhin*, which means 'sutra walk' in Japanese, is a customary practice while circumambulating a temple garden, I asked Genshu about the difference between walking and sitting meditation. He explained, 'Meditation promotes awareness, mindfulness of what is happening in the present moment. Sitting meditation helps the practitioner go deeply into the practice of awareness and understanding when practised deeply over a long period. Walking meditation helps us to practise being aware of what the body is doing and what is going on around us in the present moment. It can help us extend our practice of mindfulness into all activities. Increasing our mindfulness helps us understand the causes and effects of what we think, say and do, and how that will affect ourselves and others.'

I asked Genshu about the meaning of the Zen proverb 'From the withered tree a flower blooms.'

'Prior to starting to practise meditation regularly and deeply, a person can be like a withering tree, lacking understanding about life, its sustenance, and how to develop beneficially. With the development of meditation practice, the person can change from being like a withering tree growing older to a tree from which beautiful flowers bloom.'

On whether you need to be a Buddhist to meditate, Genshu added, 'The One who became enlightened – the Buddha – wished to help all beings come to understand things as they really are. Meditation practice assists with this. He did not set down beliefs and views for people to believe in and follow. Buddhism is not a belief system like other religions. The practice of meditation can be undertaken by anyone who wishes, and it will assist their understanding of reality.'

Cats and Zen Buddhism

Since ancient times, cats have been well respected by people in the Buddhist community and are thought to have protected the precious scriptures from pesky rodents when they arrived in Japan from China in the sixth century. As we saw in Chapter B, with the history of the *maneki-neko* at Gōtoku-ji Temple, cats have been mostly associated with good fortune. Some stories do exist, though, of cats being misunderstood by people, particularly due to their urge to hunt, as well as the folkloric story of the shapeshifting *bake-neko*, who's said to take revenge against cruel humans. Even so, in Japanese Buddhist culture, cats are most revered for their good luck, loyalty and companionship.

Unrin-ji Temple, located in Yamaguchi, about thirty minutes from Hagi city, is one place that could be revered for this positive outlook, as it is home to a famous feline story of loyalty and companionship. Similar to the Hachikō dog story made famous by the Richard Gere film *Hachiko*, this is the tale of a cat that waited loyally by his master's grave for forty-nine days after his master's death, after which the cat is said to have purposely bitten its tongue and followed his master to his grave. The cat in question belonged to Motofusa Nagai, a loyal samurai for the lord Terumoto Mōri, of the Edo period. Motofusa likely committed suicide (also an act of loyalty) when Terumoto Mōri died in Hagi in 1625. According to legend, the local cats are said to have yelled throughout the night at the news, paying their respects to the cat's loyalty. People in the local area were so impressed by the feline's devotion that they renamed the area Neko no Chou or 'The Cat's Street' in its honour.

Despite being a Rinzai Zen temple for more than 400 years (Rinzai and Sōtō are the two major Zen Buddhist sects in Japan), Unrin-ji is now politely referred to as *neko-dera*, or 'cat temple'. When I spoke with its chief priest, Jisei Sumida, about cats and Zen Buddhism, he said, 'It is difficult for humans to be happy in a complex human society, but we humans can sometimes take a cue from cats and live happily like them. It is important for humans to live wisely for a better future, or to value our beliefs and work hard. However, on the other hand, compared with the way of life in which we feel the joy of living now with our bodies and hearts like cats do, it makes me wonder which is truly superior. The more complicated our society becomes, the more we are attracted to the simple happiness that is as adorable as a cat's.'

The chief priest shared a tale, which can be interpreted in various ways, that highlights the need to find inner peace and avoid looking externally. 'This is a story I heard in my Zen training days at a Zen *dōjō* in Hiroshima. I have since looked up the source of the story, but I do not know the details. However, it is a story that left a deep impression on me.

'Once upon a time, there was an old Zen master. He was teaching Zen to young soldiers. In the middle of the Zen training, young soldiers had to go to war. The young soldiers fought and fell bravely like a tiger. Upon hearing the news, the Zen master cried with regret. "I gave a young soldier the training to be brave like a tiger and did it. But I couldn't give the next level of training to survive wisely like a cat."'

One could view this to mean that while we can prepare for whatever comes our way, life may not allow for perfect planning, so it's better to be like a cat and live skilfully without overexertion and accept that what will be, will be. Or perhaps a more philosophical take on the story might be similar to 'The Thousands', in the *Dhammapada*, a collection of words and verses of the Buddha: 'Though one may conquer a thousand times a thousand men in battle, yet he indeed is the noblest victor who conquers himself.'

Cats and *zazen*

Cats can be a great example of how to live mindfully and practice *zazen*. Chief priest Jisei Sumida says, 'I don't know if cats can be trained to do *zazen*, but the cat I had when I was a monk in Hiroshima would often sit with me during *zazen* time.'

From a neuroanatomy perspective, the cat's typical mental state has been likened to the state some humans experience in transcendental meditation. I spoke to Margarita Steinhardt, wild cat researcher and founder of 'The Wildlife Diaries' blog, about this interesting finding, as well as the proposition that cats might be intentionally meditating. Firstly, Margarita highlights that meditation itself is difficult to define, but suggests 'if it is simply being in the here and now, then it's likely that cats do' experience this. However, she continues, 'the problem, philosophically, is that we can never really know what it's like inside an animal's head because we can never escape our human perspective. So I can imagine what it's like for me to be a cat, but I can never know what it's like for a cat to be a cat.' Because it's not possible to make assumptions about the intentions of a cat, it remains to be seen whether or not they are practising *zazen* or if it's just a natural part of their being.

While more research on cat cognition is needed, some studies have found that cats emit a higher degree of alpha brainwaves than other animals and spend most of their waking lives in this state. Leading brain researcher Niels Birbaumer writes:

> The brain of a dozing cat is recognisable by its production of what we call alpha waves. The human brain is also capable of producing such waves, for example when we lie relaxing in the grass with our eyes closed. We may not be quite as skilled at this as a cat, but we can do it.

Alpha-wave activity in humans, which is associated with a relaxed mental state, can be linked to greater focus and even, some say, intuition and psychic phenomena.

Recent research by neuroscientists suggests that increasing alpha brainwaves can help reduce symptoms of depression and increase creative thinking, similar to the positive effects of meditation pointed out to us by Genshu earlier in this chapter. While practising meditation enables us to switch off and surrender to stillness, it's important to surrender the urge to compete or seek perfection. As twentieth-century Zen master Kōdō Sawaki once said, '*Zazen* never becomes anything special, no matter how long you practice.'

*

Whether or not cats experience meditation the way we do is up for debate, but one thing many agree on is that practising *zazen* with a kitty by your side is not only good for you but good for them too.

Afterword

'It looks like it's full, but in fact, it's empty.'

This was the Zen response given by the wise feline of *The Cat Who Saved Books*, a story by Japanese author Sōsuke Natsukawa. These words are uttered in response to a room filled with stuff, and suggest that how things appear may not be how they necessarily are.

This contrast can often be the cause of our interpersonal differences. Your perspective on the world is likely to be different from that of others, and positioning yourself to understand the world through the eyes of another will always be limited by the scope of preexisting knowledge. In the words of wild cat researcher Margarita Steinhardt from the last chapter, 'I can imagine what it's like for me to be a cat, but I can never know what it's like for a cat to be a cat.' It would seem that no matter how much we try to get a grasp on what's real, there will forever remain a gap between reality and perception. That said, it becomes worth considering whether the labels we apply and the stories we tell ourselves about the world, the people we meet and who we believe ourselves to be, are actually causing us more suffering rather than adding clarity to our lives. This can be a daunting thought, because when we shed our labels or free ourselves from ideologies, what are we left with? Is it possible for us to live without these assumptions, emptying our mind of the stresses that arise from our attachments to individual truth?

For instance, at first glance the life of a pampered puss might appear empty, lacking purpose or strife – day after day of long naps and belly tickles, without a care in the world. But empty and full can be two sides of the same coin or two different versions of the same reality. Could this life also be full of potential? Or love? Or peace?

Since the letters L, Q, V and X do not exist in the Japanese language, this book is missing four chapters. It might be worth considering, however, whether these chapters are in fact missing and therefore empty, or if this discrepancy has given me the potential to explore the themes of this book with greater agency. As famed Tokyo graphic designer Kenya Hara says, 'Emptiness, irrespective of who uses it and how, is the pursuit of ultimate freedom.' Not worrying about the constraints of the traditional Roman alphabet that I'm so used to gave me an opportunity to exercise creative freedom and personal expression.

The word 'emptiness' can be misleading, as we automatically think of it as nothingness. When I became aware that there were other translations of this concept that meant 'boundless' or 'infinite creativity', I was better able to understand what was being taught by various Buddhist teachers. Japanese American Buddhist monk, writer and scholar D.T. Suzuki said, 'Emptiness which is conceptually liable to be mistaken for sheer nothingness is in fact the reservoir of infinite possibilities.'

As we saw in Chapter T, words and labels can be harmful and create mental suffering if used in the wrong way. Using them can help us to navigate our world, but it's important to stay mindful and remain cautious so that we don't cling to them. Many Zen Buddhist teachers speak of being empty of the self by having no labels, no self or no ego, but also being full of potential. It's the self-centredness within each of us that we need to challenge.

When I first arrived in Japan, I struggled with the way things were done, and immediately assumed my Western way of doing things was better. But as time passed and I became more immersed in the culture I was living in, I was able to see that it wasn't a case of which was better or worse, they were just different. If we are to experience all that life has to offer, perhaps we need to avoid applying our own inherent values to others and see the beauty that surrounds us for what it is rather than what we think it ought to be. This relates to what I believe anthropology academics refer to as the emic perspective: behaviours and beliefs that are meaningful to the people who belong to that culture (i.e. how people perceive their own cultural experiences). The things I learned through being away from my own country showed me a new way of being and opened up an alternative way of seeing the world, which continues to help me to this day.

After I began to change my fixed way of thinking, my life started to flow more naturally, catapulting me through a string of serendipities that led me to finding my *ikigai* as a writer – a revelation that I believe better equipped me to handle life's challenges. Perhaps, by rescuing a homeless kitten all those years ago back in Japan, I was steered towards a place where I could begin to rescue myself. Suffice to say, while the journey of life is never an easy ride, and every so often we can be given a harsh reminder of the vulnerability of existence, for me, this new perspective equipped me to deal with what was coming next.

As I sat in the clinic waiting room for five hours, test after test was performed, and the longer I waited the more I knew the news wasn't good. Two ladies opposite me kept fidgeting with their phones, looking for any type of distraction from the unwanted news they were about to hear. I noticed as they came back from the consulting rooms that the colour had drained from their cheeks. To take my mind off the situation, I started researching the beginnings of what was to become Chapter G on *ganbaru*, a term often used for encouragement, especially when something is particularly challenging or unpleasant. Quite aptly, this chapter served as a tool in my recovery kit, as both a happy diversion and an encouraging reminder. Being receptive and open allowed me to deal with these circumstances in a far better way than I may previously have done. My mind was taken somewhere else, to a place of perseverance and strength. No one wants to hear the words 'breast cancer', but having something to focus on helped me to stay present and eased the distress I was experiencing.

Even so, there were times over that last year when I just wanted to give up and cry. Just after my surgery for breast cancer and two days after my birthday, my beloved ten-year-old cat Lulu passed away suddenly from a blood clot. It felt like an enormous bullet train had rammed right through my life, disrupting the normal happy equilibrium I had created for myself and my partner. Shortly after the tragic passing of Lulu, we had to move out of the place we were renting and were unable to properly grieve as we quickly uprooted our lives. I tried my best to embrace the teachings of *ganbaru* and keep at it, in the hope that one day this dark period would pass. To accomplish an objective, particularly in the face of adversity, is at the heart of the *ganbaru* spirit. So I kept focused on writing the chapters with the support and talent of my former marketing assistant apprentice and now friend Tina Williams, who would gently remind me if something wasn't working; and of Chie Tokuyama, my former student who now feels like a sister, who was on hand to answer any cultural questions late at night or early in the morning.

I believe that the way we react to things can have some of the most significant ramifications for how we live our lives. As we have seen throughout this book, there can be many differences between the way things appear and the way they actually are. Although we can sometimes feel burdened by a barrage of unfortunate events, the reality we live in is mostly forged within our own minds. We have little control over many of the things that happen during our existence, but what we do possess is the ability and the authority to choose how we respond.

By attempting to transform adversity into something positive we can help ourselves overcome the darkest moments in our life. Writing this book gave me the strength and focus to push on, despite the hard times I was facing. While the word *ganbaru* ought to be used sparingly for those dealing with grief or illness, at the time of writing this book, it gave me hope and an opportunity for transformation through being creative rather than reactive.

As Shunryū Suzuki says, 'The true purpose of Zen is to see things as they are, to observe things as they are, and to let everything go as it goes . . . Or as our Zen cats teach us, the important thing is to stop worrying so much about the things we can't control, and just let things be, and unfold naturally.'

Acknowledgements

I couldn't have completed this book without so many generous people, but firstly, I'd like to mention three of them. To Tina Williams, I want to thank you for your support and enthusiasm for this project and making everything sound better. Your early edits and suggestions have made the whole process so much more enjoyable. To my former student and now good friend Chie Tokuyama, thanks for being on hand day and night to answer my constant questions about Japanese language and culture. And to Minuella Chapman, whose encouragement never wanes, and whose gentle suggestions of rewording a sentence have helped me to no end. To Michiyo Miyake from Uguisu, thanks for sharing your expertise on language, culture and translation.

Thank you to the Cairns Japanese diaspora for generously sharing their wisdom, knowledge and time, in particular Jun Tagami and Masayo Miyabi Kurimoto for introducing me to the amazing Tsushima; Mayumi Kojima and her blueberry-eating cat Milky Boy for their insights; Aimi Kojimi for our special times together; Yuri Bush for reigniting my love of yoga; and Beth Hartig for introducing me to yin yoga at a time in my life I needed it most. Thanks to Rachel Carroll, whom I met on a mountain in Fukushima, Japan, in 2006 and have stayed mates with ever since.

To all the amazing people at the Khacho Yulo Ling Buddhist Centre in Cairns, and the wonderful teachings of Venerable Rinchen, Quentin Genshu and Open Way Zen, thank you. I miss you all.

During my research for this book, some people appeared at exactly the right time when I was working on a chapter. I'd like to say a special thank you to Shigeo Kondo-Maher, Yukari Sato and Dr Richard Kelly in the UK.

In Japan, I'd like to thank my friends Yasuhiro Iijima in Tokyo, and the people (and cats) of Takayama Gifu-ken for being inspirational, especially Nolico Suzuki and her old friend Hiroko Shimada, whom I mysteriously met on separate occasions on different continents ten years apart.

To the feline experts quoted in this book, a special mention to Allison Hunter-Frederick in the United States for sharing her knowledge on cat behaviour, and to Margarita Steinhart in Australia for her expertise on wild cats.

To the amazing team at Pan Macmillan Australia, firstly to Cate Blake for her enthusiasm and belief in the book during its early stages, to Nicola Young for her great copy edits and fine attention to detail, to Danielle Walker for her edits and answering all my questions, to Jane Watkins for making me smile, and completely getting what I was saying without the need to explain, and to Andy Warren for the cute feline-themed cover.

To the cat monks, past, present and future, thanks for your insights and wisdom.

And thanks to my partner, Roland Walker, for his support and sharing his humorous feline observations.

Endnotes

A | *Annei*: Peace and tranquillity

6   Article 28 of the imperial constitution says . . . : 'The Constitution of Japan,' Prime Minister of Japan and His Cabinet, accessed 8 October 2022, japan.kantei.go.jp/constitution_and_government_of_japan/constitution_e.html

7   Only about 20 centimetres long, *Nemuri-neko* . . . : Fred Cherrygarden, '"Nemuri-Neko" ("The Sleeping Cat"),' *Atlas Obscura*, 8 August 2020, atlasobscura.com/places/nemuri-neko-sleeping-cat

8   Each pole bears the words 'May Peace Prevail on Earth' . . . : 'Peace Pole Project,' May Peace Prevail on Earth International, last modified 2020, worldpeace.org/peacepoleproject

8   Goi urged people to seek inner peace . . . : 'Byakko Shinko Kai: May Peace Prevail on Earth,' Byakko Shinko Kai, accessed 28 January 2023, byakko.or.jp/about/teaching

9   Yuka Nakamura, an origami teacher originally from Tokyo . . . : Yuka Nakamura, in discussion with the author, Cairns (Australia), October 2022

10   The steel crane, welded from World Trade Center debris . . . :
      Ari Beser, 'How Paper Cranes Became a Symbol of Healing
      in Japan,' *National Geographic* (blog), 28 August 2015, blog.
      nationalgeographic.org/2015/08/28/how-paper-cranes-
      became-a-symbol-of-healing-in-japan

12   Tōru Hashimoto told me . . . : Tōru Hashimoto, in discussion
      with the author, Koyuki's owner at Nyan Nyan Ji Temple,
      August 2022

B | *Bimbōshō*: Poor man's mind

18   Studies show that people who think more positively . . . :
      Alan Rozanski, Chirag Bavishi, Laura D. Kubansky et al.,
      'Association of Optimism with Cardiovascular Events
      and All-cause Mortality: A Systematic Review and Meta-
      analysis,' *JAMA Network Open*, vol. 2, no. 9, 2019, article no.
      e1912200, jamanetwork.com/journals/jamanetworkopen/full
      article/2752100

19   Famed Japanese novelist Sōseki Natsume wrote . . . : Sōseki
      Natsume, *I Am a Cat*, translated by Aiko Ito & Graeme
      Wilson, Rutland, VT: Tuttle Publishing, 2001 (first published
      1906)

20   Aimi Kojima, a fellow feline fanatic . . . : Aimi Kojima, in
      discussion with the author, Cairns (Australia), February
      2022

21   Traditionally, Shinto and Buddhist worshippers would use
      ema . . . : Mark Brazil, 'Japanese Culture: Ema 絵馬,' Japan
      Experience, 28 December 2012, japanvisitor.com/japan-
      house-home/ema

C | *Chōwa*: Balance and harmony

27   It's said that 'they formed a natural alliance . . . ': Jean
      Campbell Cooper, *Yin & Yang: The Taoist Harmony of
      Opposites*, Wellingborough, UK: Aquarian Press, 1981

27   Cat fan and famed scholar D.T. Suzuki . . . : Dwight
      Goddard, *A Buddhist Bible: History of Early Zen Buddhism,
      Self-Realisation of Noble Wisdom, The Diamond Sutra, The*

Prajna Paramita Sutra, The Sutra of the Sixth Patriarch, London: Forgotten Books, 2007 (first published 1932)

28 ... in his book *The Training of the Zen Buddhist Monk* ...: Daisetz Teitaro Suzuki, *The Training of the Zen Buddhist Monk*, New York: University Books, 1965

29 According to Taoism ...: Campbell Cooper 1981, *op. cit.*

29 Even as far back as the ninth century ...: Yuri Ogata, 'うちの黒猫がかわいすぎる！猫好きブロガーもびっくりの溺愛ぶり、宇多天皇の日記の中身とは？' [My Black Cat is Too Cute! What is the Content of Emperor Uda's Diary, Which Surprises Even Cat-Loving Bloggers?], Warakuweb (culture blog), 9 September 2020, intojapanwaraku.com/culture/115326

31 On the subject of maintaining balance, Japanese Australian yoga teacher Yuri Bush suggests ...: Yuri Bush, in discussion with the author, Cairns (Australia), February 2022

32 As Akemi Tanaka in her book ...: Akemi Tanaka, *The Power of Chōwa: Finding Your Inner Strength Through the Japanese Concept of Balance and Harmony*, New York: Harper Design, 2020, (first published as *The Power of Chōwa: Finding Your Balance Using the Japanese Wisdom of Chōwa*, 2019)

33 Incidentally, according to findings by the Organisation for Economic Co-operation and Development ...: 'Italy', OECD Better Life Index, accessed 1 February 2023, oecdbetterlifeindex.org/countries/Italy

D | *Datsuzoku*: Break from routine

35 *Datsuzoku* is one of the Seven Aesthetic Principles of *wabi-sabi* ...: Robyn Griggs Lawrence, *Simply Imperfect: Revisiting the Wabi-Sabi House*, Gabriola Island, Canada: New Society Publishers, 2011

38 Japanese artist Chie Tokuyama says ...: Chie Tokuyama, in discussion with the author, remote location, November 2021

40 In his book *Letting Go: The Pathway of Surrender* ...: Dr David R. Hawkins, *Letting Go: The Pathway of Surrender*, Carlsbad, CA: Hay House, 2014 (first published 2012)

41   The late Zen master Thich Nhat Hanh said . . . : Thich Nhat Hanh, '5 Practices for Nurturing Happiness,' Lion's Roar: Buddhist Wisdom for our Time, 12 December 2022, lionsroar.com/5-practices-for-nurturing-happiness

41   In the words of cat behaviourist and TV host Jackson Galaxy . . . : Jackson Galaxy, 'My Cat from Hell,' Wikipedia, accessed 28 January 2023, wikipedia.org/wiki/My_Cat_from_Hell

E | *Enryo*: Reserved attitudes

45   Historian and author Toyoyuki Sabata says . . . : Toyoyuki Sabata, 'Komezukuri ni Nezashita Nihon no Bunka' [米づくりに根ざした日本の文化] (The Rice Cultivation Oriented Culture in Japan), in Nihon Bunka wo Saguru [日本文化を探る] (Behind Japanese Culture), Tokyo: Kodansha, 1985

45   Yasuhiro Iijima, who worked for Japan Rugby Football Union . . . : Yasuhiro Iijima, in discussion with the author, remote location, February 2022

46   Dr Yuki Hattori, Japan's leading cat vet says . . . : Dr Yuki Hattori, *What Cats Want: An Illustrated Guide for Truly Understanding Your Cat*, London: Bloomsbury Publishing, 2016

46   . . . could they be performing *ba no kūki wo yomu* . . . : 'Ba no kuuki wo yomu,' Wikipedia, accessed 29 January 2023, wikipedia.org/wiki/Ba_no_kuuki_wo_yomu

F | *Fukinsei*: Letting go of concepts

49   Orie Kawamura, from 365cat.art, is a Japanese illustrator . . . : Orie Kawamura, in discussion with the author, remote location, 26 October 2022

50   According to positive psychologist Tim Lomas . . . : 'About the Journal,' *International Journal of Wellbeing*, accessed 28 January 2023, internationaljournalofwellbeing.org

50   Described as a central tenet of the Zen aesthetic . . . : Csaba Okrona, 'Fukinsei,' The Leadership Garden Newsletter, 9 March 2022, newsletter.leadership.garden/p/fukinsei

51   Author Kelly Richman-Abdou says . . .: Kelly Richman-Abdou, 'Kintsugi: The Centuries-old Art of Repairing Broken Pottery with Gold,' *My Modern Met*, 5 March 2022, mymodernmet.com/kintsugi-kintsukuroi

G | *Ganbaru*: Doing one's best

55   The verb, *ganbaru*, according to Yasutaka Sai . . . : Yasutaka Sai and Erdener Kaynak, *The Eight Core Values of the Japanese Businessman: Toward an Understanding of Japanese Management*, New York: International Business Press, 1995

56   It's been reported that around 80 per cent . . . : Fran Simone, 'Negative Self-Talk: Don't Let It Overwhelm You,' *Psychology Today*, 4 December 2017, psychologytoday.com/au/blog/family-affair/201712/negative-self-talk-dont-let-it-overwhelm-you

57   Despite the usefulness behind the concept of *ganbaru* . . . : Colin P. A. Jones, 'Too Much "Ganbaru" Could Push Anyone Over the Edge,' *The Japan Times*, 8 June 2015, japantimes.co.jp/life/2015/06/08/language/much-push-anyone-edge

57   The Japanese are said to resort often to the idea of *mujō* . . . : Susan Meehan, 'Sketch of Mujo (無常素描),' *The Japan Society* (Review), accessed 30 January 2023, japansociety.org.uk/review?review=322

57   While most 'Westerners [seek] beauty . . . ': 'Mujo (Absence of Absolutes),' Japanese Wiki Corpus, accessed 29 January 2023, japanese-wiki-corpus.org/culture/Mujo%20(absence%20of%20absolutes).html

58   Kenkō Yoshida, a Japanese monk, writing . . . : Eric Weiner, *The Socrates Express: In Search of Life Lessons from Dead Philosophers*, New York: Avid Reader Press, 2020

58   In the story *Neko wo egaita shōnen*, a popular Japanese fairy tale . . . : Sarah Aswell, 'The Boy Who Drew Cats,' Stories Retold, YouTube, 30 October 2019, youtube.com/watch?v=AZSGY1gIRNA

H | *Hara hachi bu*: 'Eighty per cent is perfect!'

63 It's said to have originated in the book on Zen Buddhism . . . : Héctor García and Francesc Miralles, translated by Heather Clearly, *Ikigai: The Japanese Secret to a Long and Happy Life*, London: Penguin, 2017

64 According to one report, in Japan, approximately 56 per cent . . . : Arai Toshiro, Nobuko Mori, Yuki Okada, et al., 'Overall Prevalence of Feline Overweight/Obesity in Japan as Determined From a Cross-Sectional Sample Pool of Healthy Veterinary Clinic-Visiting Cats in Japan,' *Turkish Journal of Veterinary and Animal Sciences*, vol. 40, no. 3, 2016, pp. 304–12, journals.tubitak.gov.tr/veterinary/vol40/iss3/7

64 It's reported that 890 million people . . . : 'Number of Obese People in the World Right Now,' The World Counts, accessed 20 March 2023, theworldcounts.com/challenges/people-and-poverty/hunger-and-obesity/statistics-about-obesity

64 . . . and childhood obesity is expected to increase . . . : 'Metabolic Health: A Priority for the Post-Pandemic Era,' *The Lancet Diabetes & Endocrinology* vol. 9, no. 4, 2021, p. 189, doi.org/10.1016/s2213-8587(21)00058-9

64 It is, however, a remarkably smaller problem than in other countries . . . : Palash R. Gosh, 'Japan Has Many Problems, But Obesity Isn't One of Them,' *International Business Times*, 25 January 2013, ibtimes.com/japan-has-many-problems-obesity-isnt-one-them-1038090

65 Many studies have been done on these so-called Blue Zones . . . : 'History of Blue Zones,' Blue Zones, 20 April 2021, bluezones.com/about/history

66 A Japanese study of type 2 diabetics has shown . . . : Agence France-Presse, 'Why You Should Eat Slowly if you Want to Lose Weight – To Give Your Stomach Time to Signal to the Brain That It's Full,' *South China Morning Post*, 16 February 2018, scmp.com/lifestyle/health-beauty/article/2133345/why-you-should-eat-slowly-if-you-want-lose-weight-give-your

66   In an undomesticated habitat, where food is not widely available . . . : Intelligent Cat Care Blog, 'The Evidence for Frequent Feeding of Cats to Promote Positive Welfare,' International Cat Care, 10 February 2021, icatcare.org/the-evidence-for-frequent-feeding-of-cats-to-promote-positive-welfare

67   According to George Ohsawa, too much yin or yang in our food . . . : Cornelia Aihara and Sandy Rothman, *The First Macrobiotic Cookbook*, edited by Laurel Ruggles Oroville, CA: George Ohsawa Macrobiotic Foundation, 1985 (first published 1964)

68   Mayumi Nishimura, who worked as Madonna's private macrobiotic chef . . . : Mayumi Nishimura, *Mayumi's Kitchen: Macrobiotic Cooking for Body and Soul*, Otowa, Japan: Kodansha International, 2010

69   Inspired by the Italian economist Vilfredo Pareto . . . : '9 Proven Time Management Techniques and Tools,' University of St. Augustine for Health Sciences, 3 October 2019, usa.edu/blog/time-management-techniques

69   In her book, *The 1 Day Refund* . . . : Donna McGeorge, *The 1 Day Refund: Take Back Time, Spend it Wisely*, Brisbane: Wiley, 2021

69   The Japanese word *kodawari* means . . . : Luke Balslov, 'What is Kodawari?' Exploring Kodawari (blog), 27 May 2020, exploringkodawari.blog/what-is-kodawari

71   Thirty-two times is the suggested amount . . . : Sandra Capra, 'Health Check: Should We Really Chew Each Mouthful of Food 32 Times?' *The Conversation*, 23 November 2015, theconversation.com/health-check-should-we-really-chew-each-mouthful-of-food-32-times-50956

I | *Ikigai*: Life purpose

75   Japanese author and scientist Ken Mogi writes . . . : Ken Mogi, *The Little Book of Ikigai: The Japanese Way to Finding Your Purpose in Life*, London: Quercus Publishing, 2017

76   The clips went on to launch the Japanese cat's career . . . : J.R. Ramirez, 'Maru the Cat', Know Your Meme, accessed 25 January 2023, knowyourmeme.com/memes/maru-the-cat

78   Frankl said: 'The way in which a man . . . ': Viktor E. Frankl, *Man's Search for Meaning*, Boston: Beacon Press, 1962 (first published 1959)

79   Yukari Satō was born in Kauai, Hawaii . . . : Yukari Satō, in discussion with the author, remote location, May 2022

82   Psychologist Mihaly Csikszentmihalyi, who recognised and named the concept of 'flow' . . . : Mihaly Csikszentmihalyi, *Flow: The Psychology of Optimal Experience*, London: Rider, 2002 (first published 1992)

84   The most successful feline hunter is the black-footed cat . . . : 'Most Successful Feline Predator', Guinness World Records, accessed 1 February 2023, guinnessworldrecords.com/world-records/554111-most-successful-feline-predator

85   According to one Australian study, domestic cats . . . : James Fair, 'Apex Predators in the Wild: Which Mammals are the Most Dangerous?' Discover Wildlife, 24 November 2021, discoverwildlife.com/animal-facts/mammals/hunting-success-rates-how-predators-compare

J | *Jōshiki*: Common sense

89   Nolico Suzuki, a Japanese educator, describes *jōshiki* . . . : Nolico Suzuki, in discussion with the author, remote location, July 2022

90   As Sue Shinomiya and Brian Szepkouski write in their book . . . : Sue Shinomiya and Brian Szepkouski, *Business Passport to Japan*, revised edn, Berkeley, CA: Stone Bridge Press, 2007

91   Japan is exceedingly good at returning lost property . . . : William Park and Johanna Airth, 'Why Japan is so Successful at Returning Lost Property', *BBC* (Japan 2020), 15 January 2020, bbc.com/future/article/20200114-why-japan-is-so-successful-at-returning-lost-property

92   Author Brian Bocking says honesty . . . : Brian Bocking, *The Oracles of the Three Shrines: Windows on Japanese Religion*, Abingdon, UK and New York, US: Routledge, 2013 (first published 2001)

92   British rapper, singer, songwriter and Japanese enthusiast AJ Tracey . . . : 'AJ Tracey and Big Zuu Interview Each Other,' VICE Facebook page, accessed 1 February 2023, facebook.com/VICE/videos/5418401744868265

92   It's been well documented that after the tragic events of the 2011 Tōhoku earthquake . . . : 'Why Is There no Looting in Japan after the Earthquake?' BBC News, 18 March 2011, bbc.com/news/magazine-12785802

97   The Noble Eightfold Path, perhaps the most widely known . . . : Bikshu Sangharakshita, *Vision and Transformation: An Introduction to the Buddha's Noble Eightfold Path*, Birmingham, UK: Windhorse Publications, 1990

K | *Kanso & Kokō*: Simplicity & Austerity

99   It's said that these seven pillars of *wabi-sabi* . . . : Rebecca Zissmann, 'Kanso, One of the Seven Pillars of *Wabi-Sabi*,' *Pen*, 12 November 2019, pen-online.com/culture/kanso-one-of-the-seven-pillars-of-wabi-sabi

101   Perhaps two of the best-known minimalist advocates in recent years . . . : Ryan Nicodemus and Joshua Fields Millburn (The Minimalists), 'A Rich Life with Less Stuff,' TEDx Talks, YouTube, 19 April 2014, accessed 26 January 2023, youtube.com/watch?v=GgBpyNsS-jU&ab_channel=TEDxTalks

101   In his book *Zen: The Art of Simple Living* . . . : Masuno, Shunmyō, *Zen: The Art of Simple Living*, translated by Allison Markin Powell, London: Michael Joseph, 2019

103   The method includes a range of ideas such as 'tidying by category' . . . : 'What is the KonMari Method™?' KonMari, accessed 26 January 2023, konmari.com/about-the-konmari-method

103   He describes how, after living in the same apartment for ten years . . . : Fumio Sasaki, *Goodbye, Things: On Minimalist*

Living, translated by Eriko Sugita, London: Penguin, 2017 (first published as *Goodbye Things: The New Japanese Minimalism*, 2015)

106   I asked specialist cat gift shop owner Kumi Tonooka . . . : Kumi Toonooka, in discussion with the author, remote location, 5 August 2022

107   Author and computer science professor Cal Newport . . . : Cal Newport, *Digital Minimalism: Choosing a Focused Life in a Noisy World*, London: Portfolio, 2019

108   Author Robert W.F. Taylor uses Buddhist monks . . . : Robert W.F. Taylor, *Zen Mind Zen Life: An Uncluttered Mind Leads to an Uncluttered Life*, N.P.: self-published, 2020

M | *Mottainai*: Regret over waste

112   While researching this chapter in July . . . : Jun Tagami and Masayo Kurimoto, in discussion with the author, Cairns (Australia), 4 August 2022

117   Japan also highlights environmental causes through anime films . . . : 'Princess Mononoke,' Wikipedia, accessed 23 January 2023, en.wikipedia.org/wiki/Princess_Mononoke

118   Surprisingly, despite having such a sophisticated waste-management system . . . : Claudia Giacovelli (lead author and project manager) et al., 'Single-use Plastics: A Roadmap for Sustainability,' *UN Environment/Green Policy Platform*, Nairobi: United Nations Environment Programme, June 2018, greengrowthknowledge.org/research/single-use-plastics-roadmap-sustainability

118   Little known until fairly recently, this town has made international headlines . . . : 'A Small Town Asks "Why?": Toward a Zero-Waste World', The Government of Japan, 15 April 2021, japan.go.jp/kizuna/2021/04/zero-waste_world.html

N | *Natsukashii*: Bittersweet nostalgia

124   A small Japanese study involving forty-nine domestic cats . . . : Helen Briggs, 'Cats May Be as Intelligent as Dogs,

Say Scientists,' *BBC News*, 25 January 2017, bbc.com/news/science-environment-38665057.amp

124   Additional research shows that cats can remember . . . : Nesia Amarasthi, 'Can A Cat Remember Its Owner's Name After 5 Years? This Is According to The Study,' VOI, 26 April 2022, voi.id/en/lifestyle/162000/can-a-cat-remember-its-owners-name-after-5-years-this-is-according-to-the-study

124   In the book *The Courage to be Happy* . . . : Ichiro Kishimi and Fumitake Koga, *The Courage to be Happy: True Contentment Is Within Your Power*, Sydney: Allen & Unwin, 2019 (first published 2016)

126   It was a time of devotion to visual art . . . : Murasaki Shikibu, *The Tale of Genji,* translated by Suyematz Kenchio, N.P.: self-published, 2020 (first published London: Trubner & Co., 1882)

127   Sachiko Iwayama, author of *The Events That Shaped the History of Japan* . . . : Sachiko Iwayama, *The Events That Shaped the History of Japan*, Underwood (Australia): InHouse Publishing, 2017

128   One such example is the Oscar-winning Japanese film . . . : Ryusuke Hamaguchi (director), *Drive My Car*, Bitters End, Tokyo, 2021, see www.imdb.com/title/tt14039582

129   It means 'one chance in a lifetime' . . . : 'Chanoyu Glossary,' Japanese Tea Culture (The OMOTESENKE tradition), accessed 8 October 2022, omotesenke.jp/english/chanoyu/glossary.html

O | *Oubaitōri*: Never comparing oneself

133   To find out more about the concept of *oubaitōri* . . . : Akiko Schrader, in discussion with the author, Cairns (Australia), 17 August 2022

135   In the documentary *Inside the Mind of a Cat* . . . : Andy Mitchell (director), *Inside the Mind of a Cat* (documentary film), 2022, imdb.com/title/tt21340412/

P | *Pari shōkōgun*: Dealing with disappointment

141   The term *Pari shōkōgun* or Paris syndrome . . . : Caroline Wyatt, '"Paris Syndrome" Strikes Japanese', *BBC News*, 20 December 2006, news.bbc.co.uk/1/hi/6197921.stm

141   One person who experienced Paris syndrome . . . : Shigeo Kondo-Maher, in discussion with the author, remote location, 27 July 2022

142   I spoke with Sam Fujii, the managing director of a duty-free shop . . . : Sam Fujii, in discussion with the author, remote location, 29 July 2022

143   One example is British writer Angela Carter, who wrote . . . : Angela Carter, *Fireworks*, London: Vintage, 2017 (first published 1974)

147   In the words of the Dalai Lama . . . : Travis Hellstrom (ed.), *The Dalai Lama Book of Quotes: A Collection of Speeches, Quotations, Essays and Advice from His Holiness*, New York: Hatherleigh Press, 2016

R | *Reigi*: Etiquette and manners

149   It's interesting to note that according to research, politeness . . . : Michael Haugh, 'Revisiting the Conceptualisation of Politeness in English and Japanese'. *Multilingua – Journal of Cross-cultural and Interlanguage Communication*, vol. 23, nos. 1–2, 2004, pp. 85–109, degruyter.com/document/doi/10.1515/mult.2004.009/html

150   The NHK documentary *A Cat's-Eye View of Japan* . . . : Mitsuaki Iwagō, *A Cat's-eye View of Japan* (TV program), NHK World – Japan, 24 July 2022, www3.nhk.or.jp/nhkworld/en/ondemand/program/video/catseye/?type=tvEpisode&

153   Jun Tagami from Inner Nature . . . : Jun Tagami and Masayo Kurimoto, 2022, *op. cit.*

154   I spoke with American author and cat behaviourist . . . : Allison Hunter-Frederick, in discussion with the author, remote location, 1 October 2022

S | *Seijaku & Shizen*: Stillness & Naturalness

162   I asked Tomoko Gregory, a yoga teacher . . . : Tomoko Gregory, in discussion with the author, remote location, 20 August 2022

164   Beyond the daily benefits of taking some time out for ourselves . . . : Lao-Tzu (attributed author), *In the Guiding Light of Lao Tzu: A New Translation and Commentary on the Tao Teh Ching*, translated by Henry Wei, Wheaton, IL: Theosophical Publishing House/Quest Books, 1982

164   Yet, as Jason Gregory points out in his book . . . : Jason Gregory with Foreword by Damo Mitchell, *Effortless Living: Wu-Wei and the Spontaneous State of Natural Harmony*, Vermont: Inner Traditions, 2018

168   In his book *Shibumi*, Trevanian describes . . . : Trevanian (a pseudonym of Rodney William Whitaker), *Shibumi*, New York: Ballantine Books, 1979

T | *Torimodosu*: Bouncing back

173   I spoke with Takako Saito, the owner of Asakusa Nekoen . . . : Takako Sato, in discussion with the author, remote location, 23 September 2022

176   It is the spiritual belief in the 'power of words' . . . : 'Kotodama (言霊),' Japanese Wiki Corpus, accessed 28 January 2023, japanese-wiki-corpus.org/Shinto/Kotodama.html

176   I asked Nana Tomihara, a linguist and language support officer . . . : Nana Tomihara, in discussion with the author, remote location, 22 September 2022

177   In an attempt to see just how strong harsh words can be . . . : James Felton, 'Children Were Asked to "Bully" One Plant, While Being Kind to Another. Here's What Happened to the Plants,' *IFL Science*, 10 May 2018, iflscience.com/children-were-asked-to-bully-one-plant-while-being-kind-to-another-heres-what-happened-to-the-plants-47611

178   In his book *The Hidden Messages in Water* . . . : Masaru Emoto, *The Hidden Messages in Water*, translated by

David A. Thayne, New York/Hillsboro, OR: Atria Books/ Beyond Words Publishing, 2005

178   I spoke to Rachel Carroll, a wellbeing coach . . . : Rachel Carroll, in discussion with the author, remote location, 22 October 2022

180   Certified feline behaviourist Marilyn Krieger says . . . : Sandy Robins, 'Understanding Cats: How Felines View Our Words and Actions. Learning How to Communicate with Your Cat,' PetCareRx, 22 October 2013, petcarerx.com/article/ understanding-cats-how-felines-view-our-words-and-actions/1413

180   Interesting research from a university in Tokyo . . . : Atsuko Saito, Kazutaka Shinozuka, Yuki Ito, et al., 'Domestic Cats (*Felis catus*) Discriminate Their Names From Other Words,' *Scientific Reports*, vol. 9, 2019, article no. 5394, nature.com/ articles/s41598-019-40616-4#citeas

181   *Kishi kaisei* is what is known in the Japanese language . . . : 'Investigating Japanese Four-Character Compound Words: Yojijukugo,' Wonderland Japan, WAttention, 15 June 2020, wattention.com/yojijukugo

U | *Unmei*: Destiny

183   According to an ancient Japanese tale . . . : 'Red Thread of Fate,' Wikipedia, accessed 28 January 2023, en.wikipedia. org/wiki/Red_thread_of_fate

185   The struggling model-train-themed restaurant, opened by Naoki Teraoka . . . : Kenji Tsuji, 'Images of Kittens Roaming Around Railway Diorama Save Osaka Diner,' *Asahi Shimbun*, 17 January 2021, asahi.com/ajw/articles/14070121

186   . . . such as Shōnen-ji Temple in Kyoto . . . : 'Shonenji-Temple (Called a Cat Temple),' SHONENJI-Temple Website, accessed 28 January 2023, nekodera.net/w/eng/

186   Originally from Kanagawa, Japan, Ayami Golledge . . . : Ayami Golledge, in discussion with the author, remote location, 13 October 2022

187   Jun Tagami from Inner Nature said of the red string of fate . . . : Jun Tagami, in discussion with the author, remote location, 22 August 2022

189   In the anthology *The Karma of Cats*, editor Diana Ventimiglia . . . : Ventimiglia, Diana (ed.), *The Karma of Cats: Spiritual Wisdom from Our Feline Friends*, Boulder, CO: Sounds True, 2019

189   When I asked Venerable Rinchen Kelly from the Khacho Yulo Ling Buddhist Centre . . . : Venerable Rinchen Kelly, in discussion with the author, remote location, 17 October 2023

190   In the words of one Buddhist spiritual teacher . . . : Sakyong Mipham, 'Law of Karma,' *The Times of India*, 10 April 2010, timesofindia.indiatimes.com/edit-page/law-of-karma/articleshow/5779119.cms

191   Many experts suggest that these 'recognisable patterns' . . . : 'Synchronicity: the curious science of fate,' Exploring Your Mind, 3 July 2017, exploringyourmind.com/synchronicity-the-curious-science-of-fate

191   Yuriko Sato, a Japanese Jungian psychoanalyst and psychotherapist . . . : Yuriko Sato, 'Syncronicity: A Common Reality in Japan,' Pari Center, online lecture, 21 February 2021, paricenter.com/product/synchronicity-a-common-reality-in-japan-with-yuriko-sato

W | *Wabi-sabi*: Imperfectly perfect

200   For example, Ayami Golledge . . . : Ayami Golledge, 2022, *op. cit.*

200   Tokyo-based artist Chie Tokuyama gave a slightly different take . . . : Chie Tokuyama, in discussion with the author, remote location, 15 October 2022

201   Ritual tea drinking began in China . . . : 'Tea Ceremony – Japanese Tradition,' Britannica, accessed 29 January 2023, britannica.com/topic/tea-ceremony

201   The Zen priests who encouraged the return of the spiritual element . . . : 'Murata Jukō,' Wikipedia, accessed 29 January 2023, en.wikipedia.org/wiki/Murata_Juk%C5%8D

202 I spoke with Mayumi Kojima, a naturopath and Japanese tea ceremony enthusiast . . . : Mayumi Kojima, in discussion with the author, remote location, 7 October 2022

203 Sen no Rikyū preached . . . : 'Urasenke Headquarters,' The Urasenke Foundation (San Francisco), accessed January 29, 2023, urasenke.org/tradition/kyoto.php

203 At its heart is *kissako*, which means 'drink, tea, leave' . . . : 'History of Japanese Aesthetics (1) Heian and Mono No Aware,' Zen Abundance, accessed 29 January 2023, interactiongreen.com/history-japanese-aesthetics-1-heian-mono-no-aware

207 As my friend Rachel once said, life is like those vintage slide tile puzzles . . . : Rachel Carroll, in discussion with the author, remote location, 30 November 2022

Y | *Yūgen*: Ethereal beauty

210 While the direct translation may depend on the context . . . : Christopher Chase, 'Yūgen,' Traditional Kyoto, accessed 29 January 2023, traditionalkyoto.com/culture/yugen

211 Writer Andrew R. Deane said . . . : Andrew R. Deane, 'Chapter 12: Aesthetics,' *A Japanese Garden Handbook*, North American Japanese Gardening Association, 20 December 2012, najga.org/handbook/aesthetics

211 Standing next to me onboard a night flight to Tokyo was a Japanese gentleman . . . : Yūzo Takei, in discussion with the author, remote location, 16 October 2022

212 Izumi Purnell, a Japanese remedial yoga instructor, studied Japanese classical literature . . . : Izumi Purnell, in discussion with the author, remote location, 30 October 2022

214 'To watch the sun sink behind a flower-clad hill . . . ': 'Japanese Aesthetics,' Wikipedia, accessed 30 January 2023, wikipedia.org/wiki/Japanese_aesthetics

217 'The colour of the fur is peerless . . . ': Emperor Uda, *The Kanpyō Gyoki*, translated by unknown, quoted in Zack Davisson, 'Japan's Love-Hate Relationship With Cats,' *Smithsonian Magazine*, 11 September 2020, smithsonianmag.com/arts-culture/japans-love-hate-relationship-with-cats-180975764

218   Researchers have suggested that 'animals might respond to massive amounts . . .': Hiroyuki Yamauchi et al., 'Unusual Animal Behavior Preceding the 2011 Earthquake off the Pacific Coast of Tohoku, Japan: A Way to Predict the Approach of Large Earthquakes,' *Animals*, vol. 4, no. 2, 2014, pp. 131–45, ncbi.nlm.nih.gov/pmc/articles/PMC4494383

218   Others have suggested that cats have a special sensitivity . . . : 'National Cat Day: Is it True that they Feel Earthquakes First?' ISAAC, 17 June 2022, isaacantisismica.com/en/national-day-of-the-cat-it-is-true-that-they-feel-earthquakes-first

220   It's even been reported that experiencing awe can improve physical and mental health . . . : Summer Allen, 'Eight Reasons Why Awe Makes Your Life Better,' *Greater Good Magazine*, 26 September 2018, greatergood.berkeley.edu/article/item/eight_reasons_why_awe_makes_your_life_better

220   American writer Douglas Rushkoff says . . .: Douglas Rushkoff, 'What Does It Mean to Be Human?' The Psychedelic Podcast by Third Wave, accessed March 11, 2023, https://thethirdwave.co/podcast/episode-68-douglas-rushkoff/.

Z | *Zazen*: Sitting meditation

223   Buddhist nun and author Kankyo Tannier suggests . . . : Kankyo Tannier, *The Gift of Silence: Finding Peace in a World Full of Noise*, translated by Alan Thawley, London: Yellow Kite Books, 2018

223   When I asked Zen teacher Quentin Genshu of Open Way Zen . . . : Venerable Genshu, in discussion with the author, remote location, 14 October 2022

226   Unrin-ji Temple, located in Yamaguchi, about thirty minutes from Hagi city . . . : Ichinosaka Hikaru, *An Illustrated Book on Fortune-Beckoning Cats*, translated by Radiant Links, Yamaguchi ken: Sumida/UNRINJI, 2016

226   When I spoke with its chief priest, Jisei Sumida . . . : Chief Priest Sumida Jisei, in discussion with author, remote location, 20 October 2022

228 Or perhaps a more philosophical take on the story . . . : Buddha, 'The Chapter About the Thousands,' *Dhammapada*, ancient-buddhist-texts.net/Texts-and-Translations/ Dhammapada/08-Thousands.htm

228 I spoke to Margarita Steinhardt, wild cat researcher . . . : Margarita Steinhardt, in discussion with the author, remote location, 2 January 2023

229 Leading brain researcher Niels Birbaumer writes . . . : Niels Birbaumer, 'The Wave Theory of Emptiness,' *Psychology Today*, 1 April 2019, psychologytoday.com/us/blog/empty-brain-happy-brain/201904/the-wave-theory-emptiness?amp

229 Recent research by neuroscientists suggests that increasing alpha brainwaves . . . : Christopher Bergland, 'Alpha Brain Waves Boost Creativity and Reduce Depression,' *Psychology Today*, 17 April 2015, psychologytoday.com/us/ blog/the-athletes-way/201504/alpha-brain-waves-boost-creativity-and-reduce-depression

230 As twentieth-century Zen master Kōdō Sawaki once said . . . : Kōdō Sawaki Roshi, 'To You,' *Tricycle*, 25 August 2020, tricycle.org/magazine/you

Afterword

231 'It looks like it's full, but in fact, it's empty.': Sōsuke Natsukawa, *The Cat Who Saved Books*, translated by Louise Heal Kawai, London: Picador, 2022 (first published 2021)

232 As famed Tokyo graphic designer Kenya Hara says . . . : Nadja Sayej, '5 Pieces of Wisdom from Japanese Graphic Designer Kenya Hara.' *Print – Design Inspiration*, 1 December 2016, https://www.printmag.com/design-inspiration/5-pieces-wisdom-japanese-graphic-designer-kenya-hara/

233 Japanese American Buddhist monk, writer and scholar D.T. Suzuki said . . . : Anne Barker, 'The Change Process – Embracing Emptiness,' Barker Therapy Arts, 27 April 2012, barkertherapyarts.com/the-change-process/the-change-process-embracing-*emptiness*

237 As Shunryū Suzuki says, 'The true purpose of Zen . . . ':
Shunryu Suzuki, *Zen Mind, Beginner's Mind*, edited by Trudy
Dixon, Boston: Shambhala, 2006